SPAIN
A SLOW WALK ACROSS

Walking the Camino de Santiago

Karen MANWARING

Watermelon Press
2010

PUBLISHED BY Watermelon Press,
Melbourne AUSTRALIA
info@watermelonpress.com.au

ISBN 978-0-646-54465-6
FIRST PUBLISHED November 2010
EDITION 1,500

TEXT© Karen Manwaring
PHOTOGRAPHY© Karen Manwaring & Angela Nicolettou
MAPS© Karen Manwaring & Lin Tobias
RECIPES Angela Nicolettou
DICTIONARY DEFINITIONS FROM *The Penguin English Dictionary*, 3rd ed.,
compiled by G.N. Garmonsway with Jacqueline Simpson, Penguin Books,
Harmondsworth, Middlesex, England, 1979

EDITING ASSISTANCE Peta Murray
PROOFREADING ASSISTANCE Fran Madigan
DESIGN Lin Tobias / La Bella Design
FONTS Minion, Mrs Eaves and DIN
PAPER STOCKS 135gsm Glopaque & 150gsm Mega Silk Recycled*
*By using this FSC (Forest Stewardship Council) certified paper stock we are supporting better management of the world's forests.
PRINTED & MANAGED BY Forbes Laing @ Market Printing

PRINTED IN AUSTRALIA

CONTENTS

4	About the author
5	INTRODUCTION
10	**SECTION 1: Camino Calling**
36	Recipe: ENTRÉE~*Pilgrim Scallops*
45	Recipe: ENTRÉE~*Garlic Soup*
46	**SECTION 2: Walking the Camino**
107	Recipe: MAIN~*Trout with Jamón*
108	Recipe: MAIN~*Potato Tortilla*
118	**SECTION 3: The History of the Camino**
146	Recipe: DESSERT~*Tarta de Santiago*
150	BIBLIOGRAPHY
150	SUGGESTED READING
151	SUGGESTED GUIDEBOOKS / USEFUL WEBSITES
152	Thankyou

DEDICATED TO MY PARENTS
Arch & Edna MANWARING

ABOUT THE AUTHOR:

Karen MANWARING has twice walked the Camino de Santiago across Northern Spain with her partner Angela. Karen and Angela run regular workshops on preparing to walk the Camino, where they share tips and stories from their own Camino experiences. Karen also teaches classes on the History of the Camino, Walking Meditation and Creative Writing. She is a writer and teacher and has degrees in Modern and Medieval Literature and Adult Education.

To Lucy
have a great time in France!
buen Camino
~ Karen

INTRODUCTION

pilgrim [*pil*gRim] *n* on
visits sacred places,
P. Fathers band of
England and founded
England.
pilgrimage [*pil*gRimij]
shrine *etc*; journey t
associations; (*fig*) hum

LET'S GO FOR A WALK:
using this book to imagine and prepare for your Camino

This book is not intended as a guidebook to take with you on your Camino. There are plenty of really good ones already out there (see the reading list at the end of this book for a few examples).

A Slow Walk Across Spain is the book we wish we'd had in the months before we set out on our first Camino, when we were planning and preparing. It was then that we based some important decisions on assumptions and guesswork.
Had we known a bit more about the ins and outs of walking the Camino, we would have done a few things very differently.
So, the aim of this book is to help you prepare for and plan your walk and perhaps to reflect on it when you return home.

In **SECTION 1,** I've explored those aspects of walking a Camino that are more personal than factual – more spiritual than practical. **SECTION 2** covers the practicalities of walking a Camino, from boots and packs to food and fitness. **SECTION 3** explores the quite extraordinary history of the Camino de Santiago.

I've included some of our photos and diary entries to help give you a sense of what it's like being on the road.

I've also ended each section with a recipe for a Spanish dish or two. What better reason for a get-together than heading off to walk across Spain? If you need a reason for a second celebration, then coming home again will do just nicely. Some people won't get particularly excited about watching a slide show of your journey, so it's a good idea to offer a little culinary something as a diversion.

Our experiences and advice about the Camino reflect our own walking, eating, and sleeping idiosyncrasies. Take what you find useful; and don't worry, in the end your Camino will shape itself in its own unique way.

Off to the airport for
our first Camino

Walking through the ruins of the Monastery of Saint Anthony

OPPOSITE:
The ruins of the Monastery of Saint Felix

01

CAMINO CALLING

CAMINO CALLING:
an irrational urge to walk across an unknown country

I don't remember where I first heard of the Camino de Santiago – it was probably a radio or television documentary or a newspaper article – but I do remember my reaction. Although I knew next-to-nothing about the Camino, I knew straight away that it was something I wanted to do. I filed it into the back of my mind with an 'I'm going to do that one day' label. Over the years I would hear about it every now and again and experience that same familiar feeling. It was as if the Camino was tugging at my sleeve and asking 'When are you going to get here?'

MAP:
Some of the many
Caminos de Santiago

I'd done a lot of long-distance cycle touring in my 20s, but by the time I'd reached my late 40s I was wondering if I'd ever experience that sense of exploration again. In 2003, when I was 46, probably 20 years after I first heard of the Camino, my partner Angela and I started to dream about embarking on an adventure. We talked about lots of different walking and cycling possibilities in different parts of the world. The Camino was amongst them.

The moment of decision came when Angela suggested we each write down our top three contenders. I can clearly remember the moment when we compared lists. At the top of each one was the Camino de Santiago. It was like a game of Snap. A match had been struck and we were as excited as kids.

We talked about the challenge of walking further than we'd ever imagined and of experiencing the landscape, history and culture of northern Spain. We were also motivated by the need to spend some reflective time – we ended up calling it 'emptying the hard drive' – after a few very hectic years of work and personal pressures.

From that moment, walking the Camino changed from a dream full of 'maybes' to a reality that would need planning, preparation and commitment from us both.

THE CAMINOS DE SANTIAGO

The Caminos de Santiago are a web of ancient pilgrimage routes that meander through Europe towards the cathedral of Saint James in Santiago de Compostela, just inland from the sea in north-west Spain. There are many Caminos de Santiago. 'Camino' is Spanish for 'way' or 'path' and 'Santiago' translates from the Spanish as 'Saint' (Sant) 'James' (Iago). These pilgrimage routes begin in France, Italy, Belgium, England and beyond. Some are still clearly marked and walked by modern pilgrims, although most are not as busy as they were in medieval times. However, one Camino in particular has just about surpassed its medieval popularity.

01 CAMINO CALLING

See map overleaf

THE CAMINO FRANCÉS

The Camino Francés (or French Way) is the one most referred to as the Camino de Santiago. It traverses the northern regions of Spain, from the Pyrenees in the east to Santiago de Compostela in the western region of Galicia. It's called the Camino Francés because pilgrims often begin on the French side of the Pyrenees where several of France's Caminos meet before continuing on to Santiago. For 780 or so kilometres it passes through all kinds of terrain and environment: mountains and tablelands, cities, villages and wilderness.

PREPARED? Of course we are ...

As with many first-time Camino pilgrims, Angela and I thought that this was the only Camino in existence and when we headed to Europe to walk it for the first time, we really didn't have a clue about what to expect.

A Slow Walk Across Spain

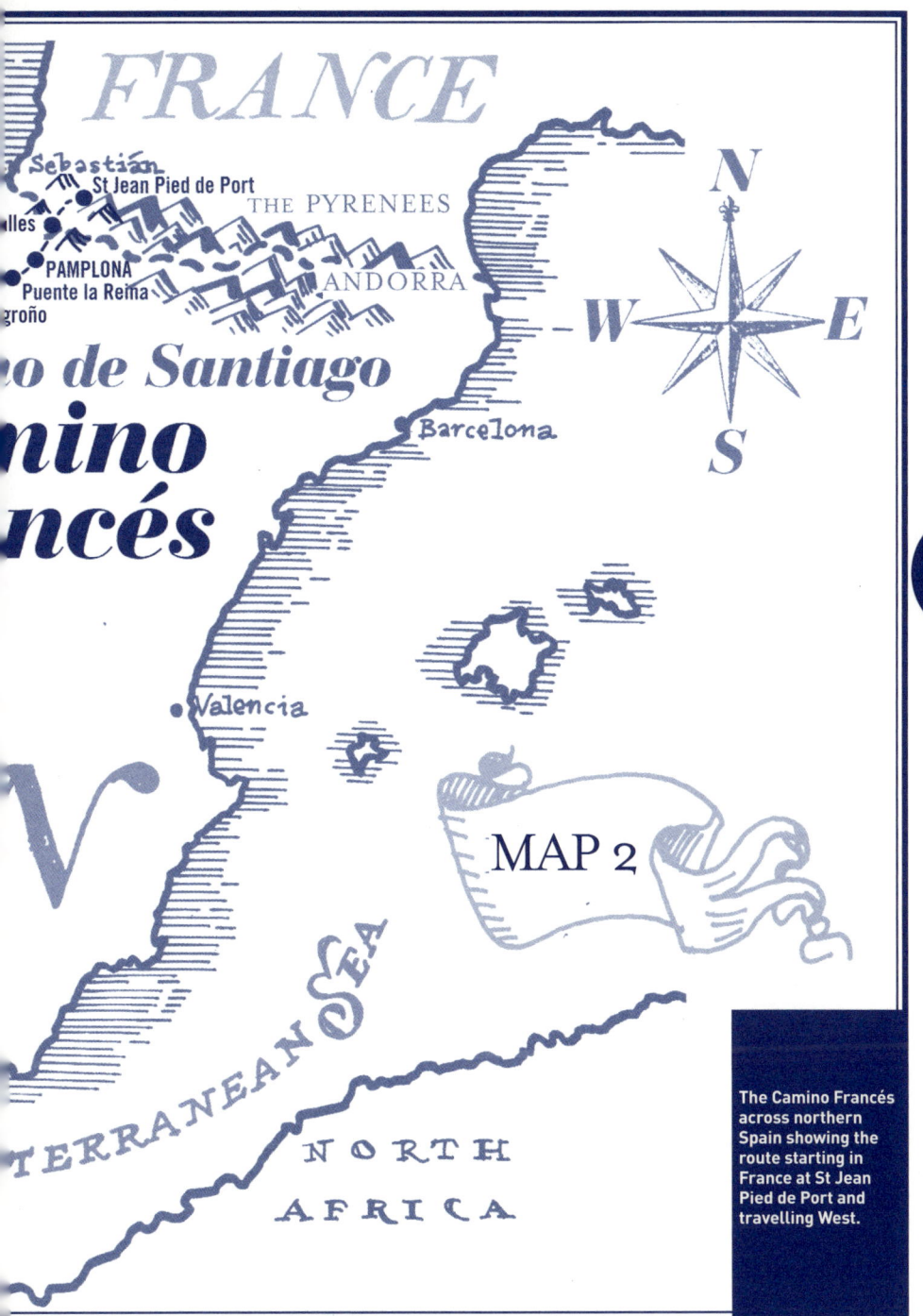

MAP 2

The Camino Francés across northern Spain showing the route starting in France at St Jean Pied de Port and travelling West.

A Slow Walk Across Spain

What we did have was a map like the one on the previous page (and the one that's at the end of this book). With the Camino de Santiago highlighted in red, it was stuck to our lounge room wall for months leading up to our departure. Again and again I'd stop and look at that wriggly red line across the north of Spain and every time, my life would re-prioritise itself. I was going to walk the Camino!

Preparation for the Camino became the focus of almost every day. It meant walking to work instead of catching the tram. Actually it meant walking just about everywhere. In the last couple of months before we left we were walking across suburbs to visit friends or to go to the movies. On weekends, we'd plan longer and longer hikes with backpacks and walking poles. Ordinary life started to feel like an exciting expedition.

As far as we knew, we were also doing pretty extensive reading and researching. We were finding websites with information and pilgrim discussion forums. They were really useful, if a little fear-inducing. 2004 was a Camino 'Holy Year', when the feast of

About to set off from Roncesvalles on our first Camino

Saint James falls on a Sunday. Many Christian pilgrims see walking the Camino in a Holy Year as doubly significant.

The pilgrim forums on the web were humming with dire predictions of thousands of pilgrims and way fewer beds. I imagined a slow conga line of tired walkers snaking its way from the Pyrenees to Santiago. Finding accommodation would be like a game of musical chairs, with everyone hovering around refuges and hostels and then pouncing on a bed the minute the music stopped. What if we couldn't find a bed?

We thought we'd better bring our own accommodation. So into our packs went a tent, sleeping bags and mats. We drew the line at a camping stove but we really did take just about everything but the kitchen sink.

Looking back now, in so many ways we weren't prepared to walk that first Camino. What a difference a bit of hindsight makes!

NIGHT AND DAY:
two very different Caminos

Angela and I walked the same Camino twice in the European springs (April/May) of 2004 and 2006. The two experiences were as different as night and day. Even though we were basically walking the same route, at the same time of year, there were a number of variables that outdid themselves in 'variableness'.

Our first Camino served us up some pretty extreme weather. Blizzards and fog alternated with baking heat and strong winds and an unforgettable 'goodbye' of a week of rain as we walked into Santiago.

Our second Camino was rather gentle in comparison. Of course we came prepared for all that we had experienced on our first trek – we even took gaiters for the snow and mud we were expecting! Instead, where we expected snow, we were warding off sunburn, and where we had panted across a shadeless flatland, we found ourselves protected by cloud. There's often an impish undertone about the Camino – as if catching you over, or under-prepared is the name of the game.

Still, the lessons we learned on that first Camino made the second journey, in some ways, easier. Being better prepared, both physically and mentally, meant we were less stressed about practicalities and more able to walk with a 'take it as it comes' mentality. That meant we could immerse ourselves a little more in the inner journey of the Camino.

THE BEAR WENT OVER THE MOUNTAIN: why walk the Camino?

We had no idea that the Camino would have long-lasting effects on both our lives, or that we would end up walking it again two years later.

The reason for walking a Camino is different for each person, but I have yet to meet anyone who has walked all or much of it, and for whom it has not signified a change.

The change may be immediate and obvious – some have returned from the Camino and upended their established life in terms of job, career, relationship or location. For many, myself included, the gift of the Camino came wrapped in a far more ordinary envelope. Inside was a calmer and wider perspective on life and all its demands, and an inner stillness that sits patiently behind life's dramas, excitements and boredoms.

It's hard to typecast a 'typical' pilgrim these days – you'll meet all kinds of people on the Camino, in terms of nationality, age, gender, motivation and personality. Like Chaucer's *Canterbury Tales*, it's all of humanity on the road.

While there are still many Christian pilgrims, modern day walkers are often motivated by the whole experience that the Camino offers. In the many Camino workshops we've run, we ask participants why they want to walk, or learn more about, the Camino.

Some people can't put their finger on a specific reason. They just feel they want or need to embark on the path. Others have a very clear motivation for walking a pilgrimage. Many are at a point in their lives where they need time out. Not just a holiday break but a dedicated stretch of time for contemplation, reflection and mental rest. Some are drawn to the Camino after facing mortality through personal illness or the loss of a partner, family member or friend. Others want to deepen a relationship by walking with a close friend or relative – or by walking alone.

The Camino winding through vineyards towards a hilltop village

If there is a common denominator it's that people think of walking a Camino as a way of stepping 'outside' of one's usual life for a bit, and so to put the habitual stresses and preoccupations aside.

The notion of consciously leaving behind one's daily life for an extended period is a very powerful one. It means recognising that what we have come to see as 'me' or 'I' is not necessarily all of who we are. There is an affirmation of curiosity, courage and adventurousness in the very concept that we can leave the train tracks of day-to-day life and walk a different path for a while.

The gift of the Camino is the opportunity to take off our mask and see what's under it, or at least to have a closer look at what it's made of. We may see that our life and its habit, the mask and clothes of established patterns, have created a persona for us. There is in this an aspect of freeing ourselves.

At the same time we can become more aware of the consciousness that lies beneath our habitual self. My experience was that I didn't have to really work at this in any particular way. The day-to-day routine of simply walking, eating and sleeping with nothing much else to distract me, did the job of allowing a sense of calm awareness to come to the fore.

No matter what the reason for setting out, it's impossible not to be affected by the spirituality and history of the path. Whatever your spiritual, psychological or religious perspective, the experience of walking a Camino has a fundamental similarity for all walkers. That similarity is the challenge of putting one foot in front of the other day after day.

SLOWING DOWN: walking the Camino as an inner journey

For most of us, stepping outside our usual life means slowing down. Although we'll probably be ramping up our daily physical exercise on the Camino, our minds have no option but to do the opposite – to do *less*. This is not how most people live – especially in cities. Generally speaking, we tend to have an over-worked mind and an underworked body. No wonder the Camino seems pretty weird at first – there's a lot of adjusting to be done, and it will take a little while.

In my case, the first few days of my first Camino made me almost unbearably aware of my mental chatter. Unless we practise meditation, we don't often stop to 'watch' our minds as they chatter away incessantly, so we're not aware of just how relentless (and often negative) our self-talk is. On the Camino, we suddenly find ourselves alone with our thoughts for fairly long stretches of time. For many people, this can be a pretty uncomfortable experience.

As each day goes by, filled with the same repetitive physical exercise, and shaped by the same routine, your mind will gradually slow down. It will observe more and think less. I found that my thinking was more about just experiencing the moment than worrying about past or future issues. When you're puffing your way up a stony incline, listening to the endless 'crunch, crunch, crunch' of your boots on the path, with nothing to plan except getting a bed and some dinner, you're not really interested in 'worrying'.

Letting go of worry for a long stretch is one of the gifts we can gratefully accept from the Camino.

Doing my best to slow down

RENEWAL: the ordinary miracle of starting anew each day

On many days, I'd make it to our destination feeling like there was no way I could possibly walk again the following day. Sore feet, big blisters, tired body. Enough. Sure, some days were worse than others but every night was wrapped in a blanket of weariness. The energy to think about tomorrow wasn't really there, so I'd go through the routine activities. Stretch. Shower. Wash clothes. Write in diary. Eat dinner. Sleep.

What I came to think of as an 'ordinary miracle' happened almost every night on the Camino. It was so simple and yet I always found it extraordinary. I'd wake up and it was a brand new day. Any left over soreness moved aside for whatever was centre stage that morning. Dancing sunlight, clear birdsong, fresh snow (a couple of times) or breakfast with Camino friends and locals. I felt so different to the way I'd felt when I went to bed that it was as though I'd been hooked up to some kind of rejuvenation machine.

I wrote this poem one morning on our first Camino:

> *Day by day*
> *to lose all will*
> *and then to*
> *gain it again*
> *to be emptied*
> *and awakened*
> *with a new reserve*
> *found in sleep*
> *drawn from the stars*
> *and the black soft night*
> *renewed*
> *blessed*
> *by the dark.*

Perhaps the extra physical demands of a Camino day made me so much more aware of the restorative effect of sleep. Or maybe I just slept more soundly on the Camino because I'd emptied my energy reserves each day.

Whatever the reason, the Camino opened my eyes to the uniqueness of each day. As the hours went by I thought less and less about reaching Santiago. More and more I felt the breadth and depth of the present moment.

One day is a very achievable thing and the Camino always brings you back to that. One day. Today.

This is another of the pilgrimage's gifts – to be aware of the journey of life as it's happening, rather than always being so focused on getting somewhere that we've almost bailed out of the present moment in anticipation of what's to come.

Waking up on an ancient path

DIGGING DEEP: building resilience

There's no getting around it, the Camino is no walk in the park. Even if limited by health or other issues to walking a smaller section of the way, or with a supported tour group, most people step well and truly outside of their comfort zone on the Camino.

The physical and mental challenges that the Camino presents can be as small as yet another boring sandwich for lunch and as overwhelming as feeling that you have to pull out of the walk altogether.

Angela and I came up against some pretty formidable situations on our Caminos. One in particular tested both of us in different ways:

> **Diary:** first Camino
>
> Yesterday we were crossing the Meseta in a heatwave. No shade whatsoever. We'd been walking about five hours. Really hard going. Heat from the sun as well as bouncing up at us from the rocky ground. Angela had started getting unusually grumpy. Earlier she'd taken one bite of her orange and spat it out saying it tasted off. She didn't want to drink either. These were signs of developing heat exhaustion but we didn't realise it. It was 7km into Sahagun and Angela later reflected that she had to concentrate on every step. We walked in silence. She said it was all she could do to put one foot in front of the other. When we got to the outskirts of Sahagun, she collapsed in the first strip of shade. I tried to bring her temperature down with a wet cloth on the back of her neck. Sips of water just got thrown up. Got her onto a train and skipped the 100km to Leon. Will stay here a couple of days while she mends.

pilgrimage [pilgRimij] n journey to a sacred spot, shrine etc; journey to a place revered for its associations; (fig) human lifetime.

Angela talks about this experience as one of the most physically and mentally difficult of her life. She remembers the absolute focus she had to call on to make each step. Psychologically she had to accept that she had no alternative but to walk until she got to shade. There was no one to pick us up, and nowhere to stop and rest. During difficult times she says that she often calls on the strength she found in those hours.

For me, apart from my concern about Angela, stepping off the Camino and getting on a train felt at the time like a personal failure. I had been determined to walk every step of the Camino. I thought I had control over that commitment. Looking back, I realise that giving in to what I couldn't control was a crucial Camino lesson. There ended up being many more but it was that one lesson that broke the back of my stubbornness. After that, things opened up a lot more in terms of my attitude.

Walking a Camino inevitably builds physical and emotional resilience, qualities that can be called on long after the shoes and backpack have been put away. Many people who've returned from a Camino talk about these after-effects unfolding over the many months, and sometimes years, later.

RUSSIAN DOLLS: a life within a life

While walking the Camino certainly meant stepping outside of my usual life, it also meant stepping into a very structured alternative. 'Camino life' is characterised by routine, ironically the thing that people are often trying to escape.

At first glance, 'Camino life' is not so different to 'work life' or 'home life': waking up, washing and dressing, getting through the day, coming home, eating and sleeping. The difference is that on the Camino, the days are devoted to one very simple and purposeful activity. Walking. Living out of a pack means that there's less 'stuff' to worry about.

Walking a Camino is like living a 'little life'. Walking through nature, whether wilderness, farmed land or the beehives of towns and cities, I became more and more aware of the natural cycles that we humans automatically reflect. With all of the usual clutter of city life pared away, the constancy of daily patterns became reassuringly clear.

Like the Russian dolls that hold ever-smaller versions of themselves, days on the Camino are each like miniature versions of the whole journey. And days on the Camino are, in most ways, the same. Rather than being boring or tiring, this repetitive routine gradually underpins the profound sense of 'groundedness' that the Camino gives.

Looking back over my diaries from the two Caminos, I can see that the experiences and reflections of these long-distance pilgrimages are like any narrative. Each day, and through the journey as a whole, they resonate with the characteristics of Beginning, Middle, and End.

IT'S ALL IN FRONT OF YOU:
the joy of starting out

Beginnings are about naivety, optimism, boundless energy and perhaps a little trepidation.

Diary: first Camino

Day 1. We left Roncesvalles at about 9am – the kind bartender at Casa Sabina sending us off with a shot of the local rocket fuel each to give us 'couragio' and strength.

It was really very good rocket fuel – a clear, light orange colour, made from local fruit. So off we went, a bit of an extra spring in our steps, and just down the road was the first Camino sign – a yellow scallop shell on a background of blue. It sent us down a beautiful path through a thick birch wood. The day was cold and a little damp and we wondered often whether the fine misty rain would turn to snow.

... and then later that same day:

We've walked through a village and then farmland and wooded mountains ... another village where it was too cold to sit for long so we ate quickly and then headed off. Made it 10kms to Viskarret/Biskaretta. That's it for today. Absolutely. Can't go on.

So much for our planned 25 kilometres per day!

YOU'VE MADE YOUR BED:
settling into the path

Middles are about reassessing assumptions as well as enjoying the freedom that experience brings. This stage is also about meeting the need for endurance, and consolidating learning. On our first Camino we really started to feel fit in the second half of the walk, after the Meseta and heading into the Cantabrian Mountains:

Diary: first Camino

The guidebook warns that 'the 50km across the mountains of Leon from Astorga to Ponferrada' is a long, hard climb. We'd been feeling anxious about this stage. The terrain map makes it look like a climbers' stage from the Tour de France. But our fitness has obviously increased over the last month and after the plodding flatness of the Meseta, these mountains are a welcome relief. We're used to pacing ourselves over demanding terrain and once we'd got into our climbing rhythm, we just enjoyed the views and the fresh air.

DOWN PACKS! Coming to a halt

Endings are a mixture of sweet and sad, relief, achievement and reflection on the journey.

Diary: second Camino

We left a bit late today, our last day of walking this Camino. The first few hours were a heady mix of exhilaration and sadness – had a few cries together. A pilgrim walking back from Santiago (!) asked us where we'd come from and we answered "St Jean Pied de Port". In a thick accent (Spanish/French/Basque?) he said "This one is for you" and clapped and bravo'ed us. I said "Gracias" and he said "Don't thank me, thank Saint James" and put his hand on his heart and made a 'for you' gesture. That was enough for Angela and I and we couldn't stop crying. But the sentimentality dried up a bit when Monte del Gozo was a long time coming and then the wet weather gear had to go on. It even hailed a little as we walked into the outskirts of Santiago.

At the end of our second Camino, this simple encounter with a pilgrim who recognised what we'd done and that we were about to finish was deeply significant to us. If it had happened near the end of our first Camino, I don't think we would have seen it that way. It would have been a nice encounter, that's all. We would still have had our concentration aimed at reaching Santiago.

The cathedral of Santiago de Compostela – the final day of our Camino

On that first Camino, we'd experienced a sense of anticlimax when we reached Santiago. Angela had half-jokingly asked, "Where's our tickertape parade?" We weren't prepared for the profound sense of ending that finishing the Camino brings. Looking back, we were a bit confounded by our feelings. We'd walked out of a green, shaded forest and into the glaring light of day. We had abruptly come to a stop, breaking the rhythm that had formed over weeks of walking. There was no emotional marker for this particular experience.

On the second Camino, we were very aware of what ending would mean. That's why a sense of sadness started to follow us a few days out of Santiago and also why the chance encounter with the pilgrim meant so much to us.

There is not only the joy of achievement but also a kind of grief in finishing the Camino. This can tap into a sense of other times of grief or ending in our lives. Don't be surprised at powerful memories, emotions or even dreams that may surface as the end of the Camino comes into sight.

THE CAMINO AS CHRISTIAN PILGRIMAGE

In the medieval heyday of the Camino, official motivation for undertaking the pilgrimage was clearly and strictly defined in religious terms – although history tells us that there were also many who were on the road for reasons less lofty.

The Christian pilgrim sought only to reach the cathedral of Santiago de Compostela in western Spain and to view the tomb of Saint James the Apostle. In the chapels, churches and cathedrals that steadily multiplied along the Camino, pilgrims could view relics and visit shrines as they travelled, and in this way they were constantly strengthening and reinforcing their faith and atoning for their sins.

You'll find more information about the Pilgrim Passport and the Compostela in SECTION 2 of this book.

The religious traditions along the Camino include the daily mass in the chapel at Roncesvalles or St Jean Pied de Port, where pilgrims are blessed as they begin their walk across Spain; obtaining a Pilgrim Passport from the local church or Pilgrim Office; the visits to the hundreds of chapels, churches and cathedrals along the Camino; and the application for the 'Compostela' on reaching Santiago.

The Compostela is a certificate granted by the Catholic Church to those who have completed the pilgrimage. Written in Latin, it is granted only to those pilgrims who, on being asked their motivation for walking the Camino, give their answer as either 'religious' or 'spiritual'. If you choose to apply for the Compostela, you'll need to visit the Pilgrim Office near the cathedral in Santiago and show your Pilgrim Passport.

Whether or not you are religious, the chapels, churches and cathedrals along the Camino are a powerful support for the spirituality of the Camino. They offer a welcome space for quiet contemplation and rest that is a perfect complement to walking the trail.

SECTION 3 – the History section – of this book gives a wider context to the origins of the Camino.

A message to passing pilgrims from the people of Villares

Pilgrim : We, The men and women of the villages of Villares, welcome you and offer you our hospitality. May our well-wishing accompany you along the way and may you always remember your journey through our land where you trod lost in thought, far from your destination.

BUEN CAMINO!
The pilgrim connection

One of the things that helped temper the challenges of the Camino for me was the sense of connectedness with other pilgrims. I felt this even towards those I never met. Knowing that there were hundreds of other people sharing the journey each day, and that millions had walked that same path before me, made my connection with this inner journey even stronger.

There is a very hardy bond between pilgrims on the Camino and every day there was evidence of it. Many pilgrims leave messages for those coming along behind. Sometimes it's a note tacked to a tree or a crayon drawing on a stone. Here and there along the Camino are cairns created by pilgrims adding a stone as they pass.

It's not just fellow pilgrims who lend support along the way. The people living in the towns and villages of the Camino will call a "Buen Camino" or show their sentiments in a more permanent way.

It's very difficult to express the nature of the 'inner journey' of walking a Camino. Difficulty would give way to arrogance if I assumed that everyone's experience would be the same. I hope though, that this section has offered food for thought about the potential for a psychological and spiritual adventure on the Camino.

While we're on the subject of food, here are a couple of recipes for the entrée course of a Camino dinner.

Adding a stone to a pilgrim cairn

Pilgrim Scallops
Serves 4

INGREDIENTS
12 to 16 scallops with shell
1 small onion, finely diced
1 garlic clove, finely diced
1 tsp paprika
200ml dry white wine
(or Galician albariño, for an authentic touch)
¾ cup fresh breadcrumbs
¼ cup finely chopped parsley
4 tbs olive oil
1 lemon
salt & pepper

METHOD

Remove scallops from shell and cut off any dark parts, leaving the orange coral and the white meat.

Rinse the shells and scallops to remove any sand and return to the shell.

In a heavy-based frypan heat half the olive oil and slowly cook the onion and garlic until soft.

Add the paprika, parsley and wine, and season to taste. Simmer until the liquid reduces by half.

Heat oven to 200C (390F). Place a scallop in each shell, season and add a small squeeze of lemon juice.

Cover with some of the onion mixture, sprinkle with the breadcrumbs and drizzle with olive oil.

Place on a baking tray and cook for about 8 to 10 minutes.

Serve hot as a first course.

It's hard to get lost on the Camino Francés

A Roman flood bridge on the outskirts of Castrojeréz

Good advice for those inclined to rush ... the Camino is not a marathon!

Just in case you were not sure ...

Pilgrims walk through the stunning landscape of the Camino

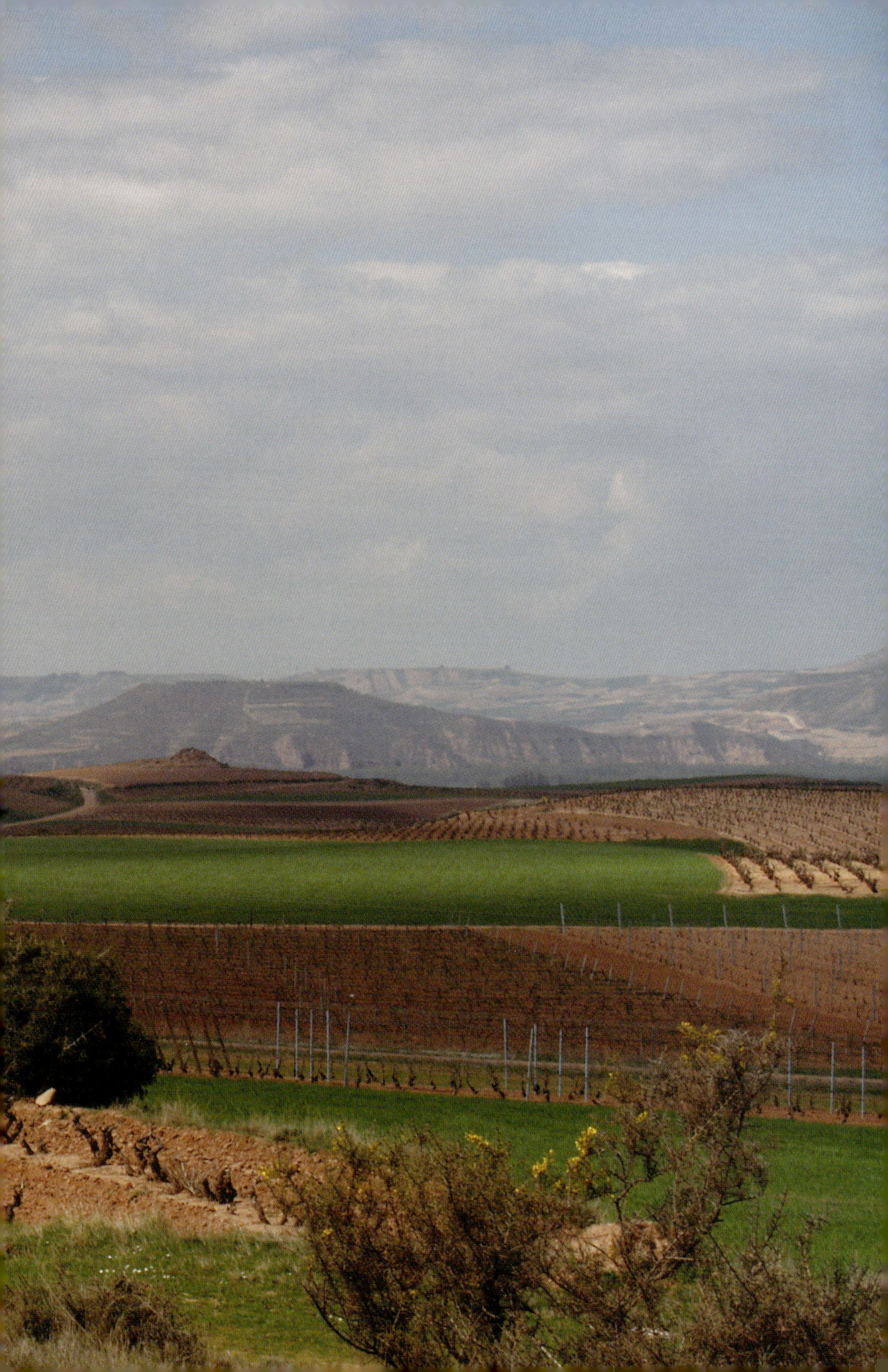

Days and days of rain in Galicia – first Camino

Snow in the Montes de Leon – first Camino

Sunny days in Galicia – second Camino

Same village (see opposite) and same time of year – second Camino

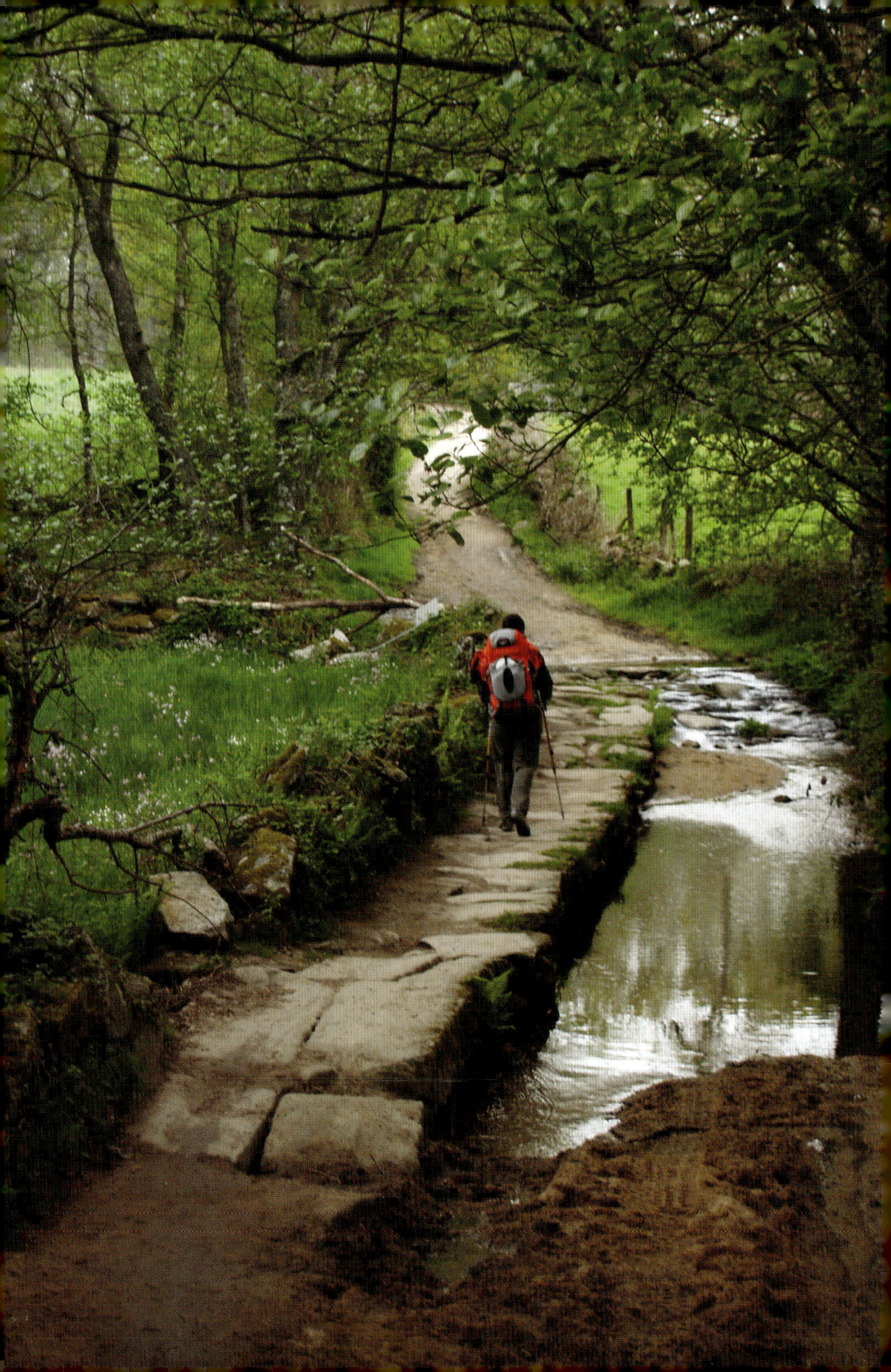

Garlic soup
Serves 4

INGREDIENTS
8 cloves garlic, chopped
1 tbs paprika (hot or mild)
¼ cup extra virgin olive oil
6 thick slices of stale sourdough bread cut into cubes
1 lt boiling water
3 eggs, lightly beaten
salt & pepper

METHOD
Heat olive oil in a heavy-based saucepan and fry the bread until golden.
Add the garlic and paprika and cook for a further minute.
Add the water, season and simmer for about 15 minutes, until the bread has broken up.
Lightly beat the eggs and stir through the soup.
Serve.

02

Walking in good company. One of the great pleasures of the Camino

WALKING THE CAMINO

WALKING THE CAMINO

The ins and outs of walking a Camino – from boots and packs to food and fitness

02 WALKING THE CAMINO

Pilgrims approaching the Meseta (tableland)

DAY AFTER DAY:
long-distance walking

Before our first Camino, we'd done quite a few bushwalks and carried packs along some pretty rocky paths. We'd woken up with tight calves and stiff shoulders with another day of walking in front of us. So we figured that walking a Camino would be fairly similar – it would just mean more of the same. How hard could that be? Really?

'Large Lesson Looming' should have been the sign that flashed before our eyes – but this is one of those signs that can only be seen in the rear-vision mirror of hindsight.

On a very long walk like the Camino, accumulation affects everything. When walking almost every day for several weeks or months, a whole new set of factors comes into play. In the first week or so, the opportunities to rest seem to diminish and stamina has yet to establish itself. This can be one of the harder bits of walking a Camino and it's helpful to expect and plan for it.

In the early days of our first Camino, it was almost impossible not to be caught up in the sheer adrenaline rush of finally being on the road after months of planning and preparation. Our bodies and minds were fresh and raring to go. We hadn't really registered just how much our packs weighed or how many kilometres we could reasonably cover in a day. Stiff muscles and joints, hotspots on our feet, or inclement weather over our physical (or psychological) landscape had not appeared on the horizon at this stage.

During that first week or so we set ourselves up for some later difficulties with a "Let's go!" attitude that was pretty uncompromising.

We learned that the antidote is to not set the bar too high – particularly when starting a Camino from a physically demanding point like the Pyrenees, the Cantabrian Mountains (just after the city of Leon) or the Meseta (just after the city of Burgos).

It's a good idea to plan to ease into a daily quota of distance and exertion. This is as much a psychological as it is a practical exercise. It's not easy to slow down when all you want to do is get going and clock up the kilometres.

On our second Camino it was easier to remind ourselves that these early days were a unique part of our Camino. We gave ourselves time to take everything in – the landscape, wildlife, villages, people and the path itself. Even though it was so tempting to set off with a bit of a race mentality, we tried to give our bodies and minds some space to get accustomed to it all.

Checking the guidebook in the Pyrenees

KNOWING WHAT'S AHEAD:
guidebooks

There are several good guidebooks to the Camino Francés (as well as to many of the other Caminos in Spain and Europe). They range from lightweight booklets that cover the essentials, through to heavier books that go into the detail of history, architecture and even the different flora and fauna of the regions.

When we were in the planning stages of our first walk, it seemed like a great idea to take along reference books that would give us the history of a particular town or statue, or the name of a flower or bird. Thankfully we resisted the urge to carry a small reference library with us.

On both Caminos we took the slim, hardy and lightweight guide to the Camino Francés (St Jean Pied de Port to Santiago de Compostela) that is published (and updated every year) by the Confraternity of Saint James in London.

In my opinion, this guide contains all the necessary information. In favour of lightness, it sticks to the basics: brief details of the route and "…its cathedrals, monasteries and churches and other buildings of special interest (and the treasures within them) that are to be found along the way."

The guide also names all towns and the distances between them, refugios as well as some private accommodation (with approximate costs, comments and sometimes, phone numbers), and a practical advice section – the 'yellow pages' – in the centre of the guidebook.

The Confraternity of Saint James (CSJ) is a non-denominational British charity devoted to supporting pilgrims and the medieval Caminos throughout Spain and France. Their guidebooks can be ordered easily online. Ours arrived within a week or two.

Another popular guidebook is John Brierley's *A Pilgrim's Guide to the Camino de Santiago*. While it is heavier than the CSJ guides, it includes a lot more information about each stage and about the Camino in general.

The contact details for the Confraternity of Saint James, as well as suggestions for a few other guidebooks, are in the reading lists at the end of this book.

ALL YOUR PAPERS IN ORDER:
the Compostela and the Pilgrim Passport

One of the few 'official rules' of the Camino de Santiago states that you have to walk at least the last 100 kilometres (or cycle the last 200 kilometres) to Santiago to qualify for a Compostela – the ornate certificate in Latin that states that you have completed the Camino. Pilgrims collect their Compostela from the well-worn Pilgrim Office, just around the corner from the cathedral in Santiago.

In any of the main towns where you begin your pilgrimage, you can collect a 'credencial de peregrino' or Pilgrim Passport. There is room on its foldout pages for the many unique and beautiful stamps or 'sellos' that can be obtained from almost every town and village along the Camino. Usually the refugio, the town hall or the local bar will have one. Sometimes, you'll get different stamps from different places in the same town.

Some pilgrims choose not to apply for the Pilgrim Passport. For most, the passport and the Compostela certificate are important mementos of the Camino.

The cathedral in Santiago has stated that from 2009 it would only accept credencials (Pilgrim Passports) issued by the church to qualify for the Compostela. (There are many 'commercial' pilgrim passports available in Spain). So if you want to make sure that your Pilgrim Passport is recognised in Santiago, make sure you obtain it from a church-affiliated source (for example, at the nearest Pilgrim Office or local church and at some refugios). You can also apply for a Pilgrim Passport from the Confraternity of Saint James if you become a member of that organisation.

Stamps in our pilgrim passport

WHEN TO GO: spring, summer, autumn or winter?

To reduce the likelihood of extreme weather conditions, spring (March, April, May) and autumn (September, October, November) are the best seasons to walk. It is also less crowded on the Camino Francés during these seasons.

The summer months of June, July and August are not only really hot but are usually very crowded on the Camino. At any time of the year the greater proportion of pilgrims are Spanish, and even more so in summer when most Spaniards take their annual holiday. Many spend one or two weeks walking, then return the following year and take up where they left off, completing their Camino over three or four years.

Lots of Spanish pilgrims walk the Camino in July and time their arrival in Santiago to coincide with the feast day of Saint James on July 25th. If you are walking at this time, remember that accommodation can be hard to come by – whether in the cheap communal refugios, or in hotels and other private accommodation.

A great number of Spanish pilgrims also want to be eligible to obtain their Compostela by walking at least the final 100 kilometres before Santiago (or cycling the final 200 kilometres). This means that many pilgrims start in the town of Sarria, 100 kilometres before Santiago. From Sarria, the Camino suddenly becomes crowded with pilgrims who look much fresher than those who've started further back! Between Sarria and Santiago, if you are staying in hotels or other private accommodation, it's wise to book ahead (you can't book a bed in a traditional refugio – it's first-come, first-served).

The summer rise in pilgrim numbers mirrors the rise in temperature. The heat can be extreme, particularly on the Meseta or high tableland, which is roughly the middle part of the Camino Francés, between the cities of Burgos and Leon. Shade and water are hard to come by, and distances between villages are longer (about 17.5 kilometres is the maximum) on the Meseta.

We made sure we were well hydrated before we began walking each day and that we carried enough water to get to the next town. This is even more important in the summer months. At the hottest times, pilgrims need to drink at least a litre of water an hour between towns. Most summer pilgrims begin walking very early, often before sunrise, so that they can rest during the hottest part of the day.

We started our first Camino in early April and reached Santiago in mid-May. If you also decide to walk the Camino in the spring, you'll experience the week of Easter ('Semana Santa' or 'Holy Week') and its festivities, including whole villages parading through the streets with statues of Jesus and Mary.

Diary: second Camino

A rest day in Burgos today. Walked around town looking for a supermarket for tomorrow's supplies but all closed for Easter Thursday. In the afternoon we joined hundreds of people in front of the cathedral to watch the first of many Easter parades. There were groups, sort of like marching bands, dressed in different colours but always in the same style – outfits that haven't changed for centuries and that looked unsettlingly like Ku Klux Klan outfits to us. I think they are mourning garb for the suffering and death of Christ. Statues of Jesus and Mary carried on floats (with about 10 people supporting each float from beneath – their feet just visible below the cloth-covered sides). Jesus and Mary's floats approached from opposite sides of the cathedral and met in front – all to the slow, mournful beating of drums. This all continued at a snail's pace from afternoon until nightfall and there was no hope of moving until it was all over, the crowd was so thick.

Accommodation is often scarce during Semana Santa. If you're staying in private accommodation, it's one of the few times when booking ahead is advisable.

Also in spring, the Spanish celebrate their version of 'May Day'. We walked through mountain villages where huge bunches of wildflowers hung above every door and along the second storey balconies lining the narrow, cobbled streets. It was as if we had travelled back to medieval times.

In the autumn months, the young, green wheat of spring is transformed into tall, golden fields and the grapevines are heavy with fruit. Much of the forests too, are turning to red and gold as they prepare to drop their leaves for the winter. Autumn is another time when the weather is likely (although not certain) to be less extreme.

As the Camino becomes more popular, those pilgrims seeking a more solitary experience (or a greater challenge) are choosing to walk during the winter. The Confraternity of Saint James publishes a winter guide that gives essential information, such as which refugios and other accommodation are open during the winter months. Obviously the mountainous sections of the Camino are deep in snow during winter and walkers need to be sure of their fitness, equipment, clothing and accommodation.

WHERE TO START?

There is no hard and fast rule about where to begin your Camino.

Not all pilgrims have the resources of fitness, time or funds to walk from the Pyrenees to Santiago. They may decide to walk a shorter section. Many Europeans do this, and come back at a later date to walk a further stage.

For those looking to walk only one stage of the Camino the question often asked is: "Which one is the best?"

The tricky thing is, not everyone agrees as to the "best" stage of the Camino. Put the question out there and you'll get different answers, all backed up with passionate justifications. I've heard people say things like:

> ... the crossing of the Pyrenees and the descent into the farmland and vineyards of Navarra and the Rioja regions has to be the most beautiful part of the Camino, and there are plenty of villages and towns at regular intervals so you can ease into things.

> ... the flatness of the Meseta with its endless horizon and lack of distraction is like a walking meditation.

> ... from the Cantabrian mountains into Galicia, the Camino is spectacular. The Celtic heritage of Galicia is obvious in the buildings, the music and the people's fascination with all things mystical (especially the witches!) It's where to start if you really want to finish in Santiago or Finisterre.

So, it's up to you! (*For more detailed information on the different 'sections' of the Camino, see pages 64–70*).

Given the possibility of unscheduled happenings, it's a good idea to be a little conservative when planning your timeline. Factor in a bit of extra time for the unexpected.

If you have real doubts about whether you can walk the 780 or so kilometres of the Camino Francés in the time you'd planned, you can either decide to start your Camino closer to Santiago, to take longer to complete the walk, or to take a train or bus between sections.

My idea of a perfect Camino would be to take a good few months or more, so that I had all the time I needed to explore villages and towns, and to take one of the many side-trips to ancient monasteries, castles or archaeological sites, or just to stay a few days longer in a village or city I really liked.

STARTING IN THE PYRENEES

For those who have decided to walk the Camino Francés from the Pyrenees to Santiago, the choice is a fairly simple one between two traditional starting points – St Jean Pied de Port in France, or Roncesvalles in Spain.

St Jean Pied de Port is a medieval town in the south of France, in the foothills of the Pyrenees and very close to the border of Spain. It has always been an important town on the Camino Francés as well as a traditional starting point. The local Pilgrim Office and a tourist centre provide support and information to pilgrims who are starting their Camino and there is plenty of albergue and private accommodation.

Roncesvalles, just over the border in Spain, is more a hamlet than a village, but its size doesn't match its importance in the history and legend of this region. In 778, in the Valley of Valcarlos behind Roncesvalles ('Roncevaux' in French and 'Orreaga' in the Basque language), Charlemagne was defeated and Roland, the hero of the 12th century epic poem *The Song of Roland*, met his death.

One of my favourite travel writers, Dervla Murphy, wrote that she'd wanted to visit Roncesvalles since she first saw this tiny hamlet's name. Dervla said that it was one of several names on world maps that had always inexplicably called to her.

If you are choosing between St Jean Pied de Port or Roncesvalles for the beginning of your Camino, it is important to note that, although the distance between the two towns is only about 27 kilometres, those kilometres involve a climb of some 1300 metres and the crossing of the Pyrenees.

CROSSING THE PYRENEES:
the high road or the low road?

The crossing of the Pyrenees between St Jean Pied de Port and Roncesvalles can be made in two ways. Basically it's the high road or the low road.

Heading into the Pyrenees

The High Road

The high road is known as the Napoleon Route (Napoleon took his army, wagons and pack animals over this route in the early 1800s). This route is famously beautiful with much of it above the tree line. It is also a potentially dangerous path if you don't consult with the locals in St Jean Pied de Port about expected weather conditions.

Depending on your level of fitness, you should allow up to 12 hours to complete the 25 kilometre crossing from St Jean to Roncesvalles. It is important to start early (before 9am) so that you have plenty of daylight. Make sure you also carry plenty of water as there are not many opportunities to fill your water containers. To shorten the route a little, you can walk to, and stay in Honto, the only settlement on the Napoleon Route, about five kilometres after St Jean on the path to Roncesvalles. This will reduce the length of your climb by one-and-a-half to two hours.

The Confraternity of Saint James guidebook gives clear information about the markers to follow, the distance to the village of Honto and the location of drinking water. It also gives accommodation details and advice about booking in advance.

While most relatively fit and healthy pilgrims take this route without any more problems than stiff muscles and tiredness the next day, some have become stranded and over the years, a few have lost their lives due to sudden changes in the weather.

Dense fog, snow and cold are the particular dangers at any time of the year. This is why it is absolutely essential that you let the Pilgrim Office in St Jean Pied de Port know that you intend to take the Napoleon Route and that you take their advice about the weather conditions before setting out.

If you aren't very fit or are in any way unsure about taking the Napoleon Route, then you can follow our footsteps (and those of most medieval pilgrims) and take the 'Road Route'.

The 'Road Route' through the Pyrenees

The Low Road

The alternative crossing of the Pyrenees is via the 'Road Route' – still a demanding climb but not as exposed to the elements as the Napoleon Route. The Road Route climbs up through the river valley while the Napoleon Route follows the higher ridge. This lower path doesn't get much of a mention in many of the guidebooks, although the Confraternity of Saint James guide refers to it as:

… the one followed by most medieval pilgrims and … the preferred alternative for cyclists and less fit walkers. It is the only feasible route in bad weather.

The Road Route is also not often recommended, probably because of its name, which gives the impression that you'll be sharing your walk with cars and trucks. In fact much of the Road Route is a thin, earthen track, winding upwards through beech forest. The road, when you do need to walk beside it, is relatively quiet. This route also differs from the Napoleon Route in that it passes through two picturesque Basque villages. One of them, Valcarlos, offers the possibility of breaking your journey overnight by staying at the local tavern, and taking two days to make your crossing of the Pyrenees. We took this option on our second Camino:

Diary: second Camino

Valcarlos is a beautiful Basque village, narrow to fit the valley and squeezed beside a running and bubbling river with sheer cliffs on each side. The low, strong Basque houses are built of great stones – the largest saved for the top of the front door and engraved with the year they were built – 1770, 1803. The front doors are usually split across the middle, like barn doors. The door of the tavern where we are staying is the same – a good six inches thick – with only the top half of the door open during the day. The soup for dinner was delicious and nourishing.

A Slow Walk Across Spain

Another point of interest in Valcarlos is the life-size statue of Santiago Matamoros in the local church (you can get the key from the local bar).

So it's up to you which path you take across the Pyrenees – they each have their beauty – the spectacular mountain scenery of the High Road, or the Low Road's winding path through woods and tiny mountain villages.

Just remember to always be guided by local advice when it comes to the weather.

> There is more about Santiago Matamoros in the History section of this book.

Getting to your starting point

Wherever you decide to begin walking, you'll need to work out how to get to your starting point. It's pretty much a case of finding the nearest city or large town and getting there by plane, train or bus.

On our first Camino, when we started in Roncesvalles, we decided to get ourselves to Pamplona – the nearest Spanish town that has a bus connection to Roncesvalles. We had spent a week in Barcelona before starting our Camino, so we caught a train from Barcelona to Pamplona.

Once we got to Pamplona, it was a matter of finding the bus station and the afternoon bus to Roncesvalles. Suddenly our Camino had begun.

Diary: first Camino

Waiting at the 'station autobus' in Pamplona – the little ticket window with the cracked glass was firmly shut and didn't look like opening. So we found a table at a small bar opposite and ordered a bocadillo (omelette inside a bread roll) and a drink and sat down to play cards. I don't think playing cards in public is the done thing for women – we got some funny looks.

At 6pm sharp, two buses left Pamplona station and, for an hour, climbed the hairpin bends up into the Pyrenees to reach the tiny hamlet of Roncesvalles. There was a lot of snow on the peaks in the background and big, icy drifts still unmelted here and there in the village. The most imposing of these was in the courtyard of the cloister at Roncesvalles monastery – still a good five feet deep in the enclosed space that, in this early part of Spring, is rarely touched by the sun.

We booked into a room at the Casa Sabina, one of only two small 'hostals' (hotels) in Roncesvalles. Before dinner we attended the mass for the blessing of the pilgrims in the church of the monastery. A good start to the Camino and we managed to hear the priest's reference to 'dos peregrinos de Australie' (two pilgrims from Australia) as well as the many other countries represented by pilgrims at the service.

While most pilgrims had headed for the refugio, there were still at least 30 of us who gathered in the dining room of the hostal for dinner. We sat around several large round tables and the cheery waitress deposited a giant, steaming, metal tureen in the centre of each. We ladled out as many serves of the thick potato soup as we needed, sopping it up with thick bread. As would become the norm along the Camino, earthenware jugs of red wine were constantly refilled.

A Slow Walk Across Spain

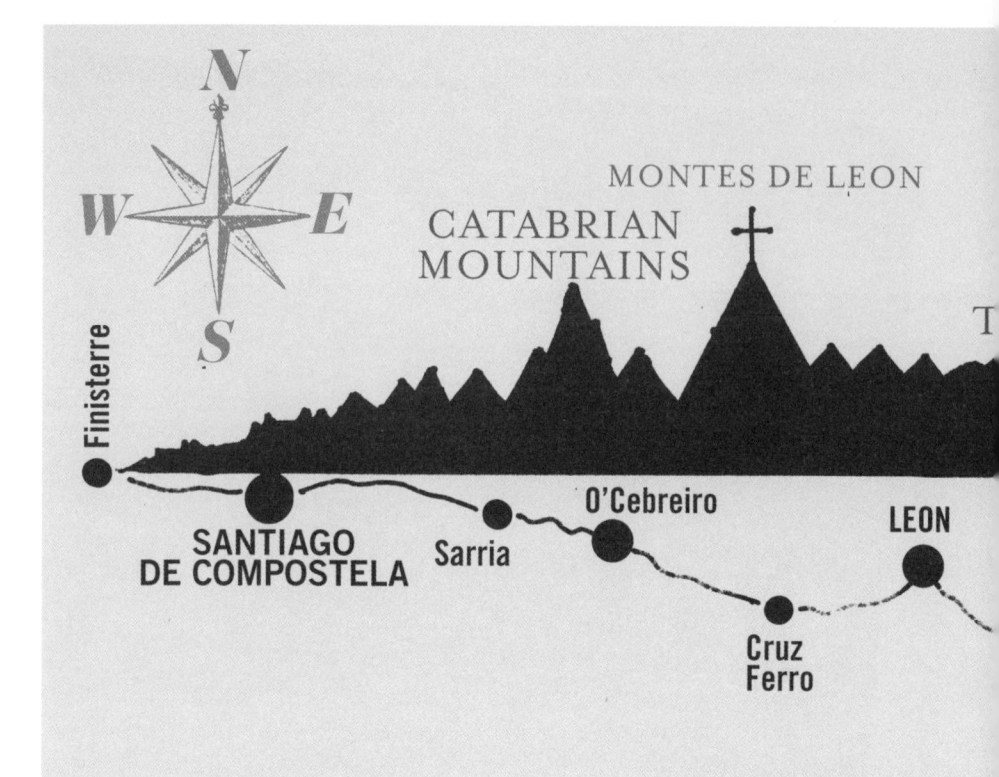

WHAT'S AHEAD?
Stages of the Camino

The elevation outline above the Camino gives an indication of the terrain.

When it comes to terrain, there are several fairly distinct sections of the Camino Francés:
- the Pyrenees
- the rolling hills, vineyards and wheatfields of the Navarra and La Rioja regions
- the high, flat tableland of the Meseta
- the Leon and the Cantabrian Mountains
- the lush, wooded region of Galicia.

You will also walk through four main cities on the Camino Francés if you begin in the Pyrenees – Pamplona, Burgos, Leon and Santiago.

PYRENEES MOUNTAINS

ETA
LAND

ALTO DEL PERDÓN

St Jean Pied de Port

Roncesvalles

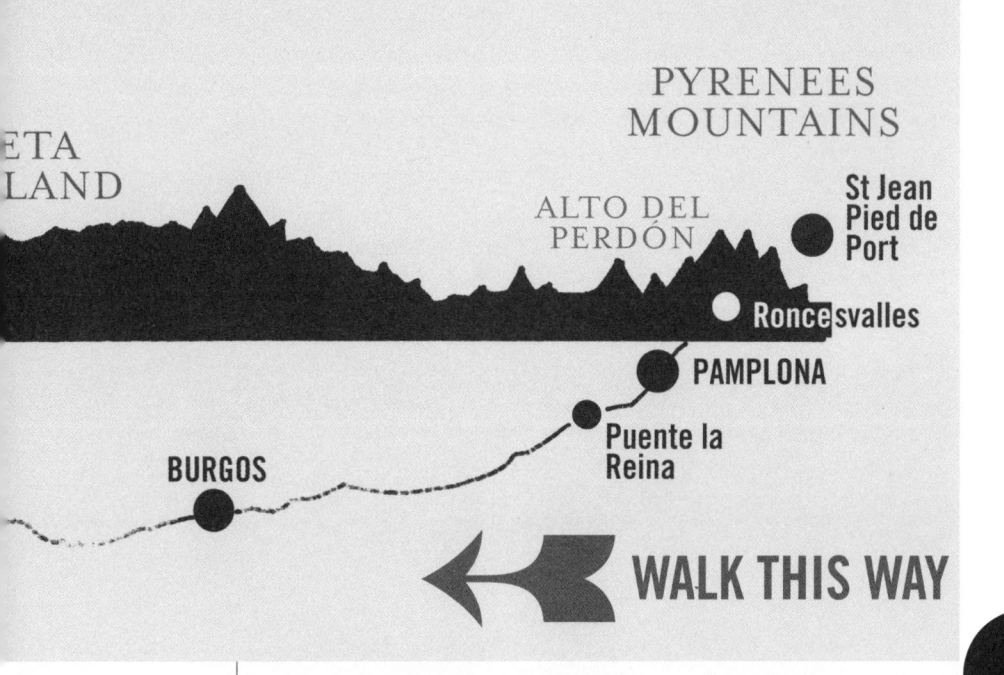

PAMPLONA

Puente la Reina

BURGOS

← WALK THIS WAY

The Pyrenees

The magnificent and somewhat mysterious Pyrenees form a natural border between France and Spain. The Camino Francés crosses the Pyrenees through the Roncesvalles Pass (also known as the Cize Pass) towards the western end of the mountain range. *(see 'Where to start' on page 56 for more information about the Pyrenees).*

Diary: second Camino

Arrived at the top of the pass of Roncesvalles where the Napoleon Route meets the low path from Valcarlos. The wind was gale force as we reached the 'top' of the Pyrenees – a saddle that gave us our first view into Spain.

Navarra and La Rioja

After the Pyrenees, your first week or so of walking is through the green rolling hills of Navarra. The Roman, Christian, Muslim, Jewish and Basque influences of this ancient region are etched in the stones and artwork of its castles, monasteries, churches and villages. This is one of the greenest regions of the Camino – at least until you get to Galicia in the west. Near the Pyrenees the hills are covered in beech, pine, oak and box forests that make for some lovely picnic stops and varied walking. The region of La Rioja is introduced by a change in the colour of the earth and the increase in the number of vineyards.

Diary: first Camino

In the autonomous region of La Rioja now, renowned for its wine. The earth has changed to a musky, mushroomy red. Vines are planted in every available flat spot, sometimes right up to the path.

The Meseta

After leaving Burgos you will begin to notice that the highest points of the landscape are becoming more and more 'flattened'. This is most evident at first in the levelled tops of the hills, with any variation in the path being a 'dipping down' rather than a climb. The terrain is forming itself into the Meseta (or tableland), an elevated plain that stretches from Burgos to Leon.

Diary: second Camino

The towns on the Meseta are strangely beautiful. Very neat and clean. All the buildings are made of either rammed earth and wooden beams, or of small, thin, rectangular bricks – handmade, every one. We also saw a few churches – hermitages – on the Meseta. Very simple and old on the outside – all locked up and seemingly abandoned. But as with much of the life and buildings in Spain and particularly on the Meseta, while the outside seems closed and dusty, the inside

> is beautiful and well-tended down to the finest detail. At one of the small, locked churches, I knelt down and looked through a crack in the bricks, expecting to see a ruined interior. I glimpsed a perfect altar with fresh, white linen and flowers and the Virgin dressed in all her glory.

There are some memorable towns on the Meseta – and plenty of space in between to think about them.

Diary: second Camino

We both felt like we were on a kind of walking 'automatic pilot' today – but in a really good way. Still can't get over how it's impossible to tell how far we've walked. Everywhere else there's a landmark to reach – a tree, a hill, an outcrop, a village, something. On the Meseta, there is almost nothing and what IS there is hidden.

I should add that the 'view for miles and miles' on the Meseta can be a deceiving one. Although the Meseta is very 'flat' it is crossed here and there with deep ravines that offer an excellent place for a village, protecting it from the extremes of the plain.

Diary: second Camino

Earlier today we experienced the weirdness of the Meseta. We would walk, and walk and walk, with the guidebook telling us the next town was supposed to be a few kilometres away – but nothing, absolutely nothing in sight. Long freight trains gliding across the horizon like toys. Just distance and space, and time seeming to stand still. Then a van passed us on the road and as we watched it travel ahead, it suddenly disappeared. Just like that – gone. Then the train disappeared. Finally we realised we were going to dip down into another 'Meseta crevice' and that hopefully the town would be in it.

On our first Camino, it was on the Meseta, just before the historic pilgrim town of Sahagun, that Angela suffered from heat exhaustion. It taught us a lesson about the Meseta – that even though it may not be extremely hot (the temperature was in the low 30s), the radiant heat from the stony ground and the lack of shade, combined with constant exercise, made for speedy dehydration.

So, a couple of tips about walking the Meseta: wear a broad-brimmed hat that shades your face and the back of your neck, and make sure you're well hydrated before and during the day's walk.

The city of Leon almost, but not quite, marks the end of the Meseta. Make sure you take the time to visit the ancient quarter. If you take a rest day here, there are some really good restaurants. The stained glass in the cathedral is world famous.

The Montes de Leon and the Cantabrians

By the time you leave Leon, you will have started to see something on the horizon that isn't a mirage – mountains! Nothing much at first, but as you walk on, the Montes de Leon introduce themselves in all their splendour. Given the contrast provided by over a week of walking the Meseta, these mountains beckon with their cool, blue outline. For much of the year, there's snow on the higher peaks.

The walled town of Astorga, with its ancient Roman origins, heralds the climb into the Montes de Leon. Astorga is famous for its chocolate and the mountains beyond will burn as much as you eat! In the following days you will reach the highest point of the Camino Francés, marked by the Cruz Ferro (or 'iron cross'). It's traditional to take a small stone from home to add to the giant cairn at the base of the cross. Just past the Cruz Ferro is the village of Manjarin and its single inhabitant – Tomas. In the tradition of the Knights Templar, he is dedicated to supporting pilgrims as they cross these mountains.

It was in these mountains that we encountered wind, snow and low cloud on our first Camino. We were warm, relatively waterproof, and the way was clearly marked, so we were able to enjoy the adventure. On our second Camino, this same section was clear and hot. So again, be prepared for anything when it comes to the weather.

No sooner have you crossed the Montes de Leon, within a day or so you begin to climb yet again. The Cantabrian mountains are a breathtaking introduction to the region of Galicia.

Galicia

There are three routes into Galicia – all leading to the beautiful mountain village of O'Cebreiro. As for all the mountain routes on the Camino, the advice is the same: if the weather is bad, take the lower route.

Whichever path you take, the climb is steep but O'Cebreiro makes it all worthwhile. Although it's become a bit touristy, this village is a preserved piece of Galicia's history. Here and there squat Galicia's Celtic dwellings (called 'pallozas'). They are small and round with stone walls, thatched roofs and very low doorways. There was a pilgrim hospital in O'Cebreiro that began tending to pilgrims in the 12th century and did not close until the mid 1800s.

Diary: second Camino

In O'Cebreiro. Found the nice tavern where we had lunch on our first Camino. As it was then, really friendly and great food. Woke up to stunning scenery. All of the mountain peaks in the distance just showing above a deep sea of cloud. It's a world above the clouds. Still a steep climb straight up and out of town.

Galicia is a region of green fields bordered by stone fences. The farms are small and seem to be mostly family concerns. The Celtic influence of the region is evident in the many Celtic crosses as well as the folk music. Souvenir witches and their brooms made of twigs are everywhere in the tourist shops. Walking through the filtered green light of the forests and ferny glades, I half expected to hear a cackle or spot an elf.

Santiago de Compostela

The last 100 kilometres into Santiago begin at the large town of Sarria. Lots of pilgrims walk only this last 100 kilometres so if you're not willing to take whatever spare space is available in the refugios, make sure that you've booked private accommodation a day or two beforehand.

The final walk into Santiago is just like walking into any modern city. The Camino passes freeways, an airport and modern suburbs for more than five kilometres and it may seem that you've left the character-filled Camino behind. Be patient, you will eventually arrive in the old city centre and then the great Plaza del Obradoiro in front of the cathedral.

After reaching Santiago de Compostela many pilgrims continue, either on foot or by bus, for a further 89 kilometres to the coastal settlement of Finisterre (Lands End). In medieval times the Atlantic coast was the end of the known world. Beyond were stormy and unchartered waters full of sea monsters and unknown dangers. Many believed that one would literally fall off the edge of the earth if they ventured into that sea.

Guidebooks list accommodation on the way to Finisterre and at the village itself. If you have the time it is well worth continuing to the coast.

THE RAIN IN SPAIN:
weather on the Camino

Weather on the Camino is, to say the least, as changeable as the terrain – no matter what the season. On the east to west journey from the Pyrenees to Santiago de Compostela, you'll cross two main mountain ranges (the Pyrenees and the Cantabrians) where snow, rain and fog can descend at any time; the rolling farm and wine country of Rioja where the weather is (usually) less extreme; the wide, flat highland of the Meseta with its extremes of heat and cold; and finally, the rain-soaked western province of Galicia, where keeping your feet dry can be a real challenge.

Having said all this, you can have the good luck to be followed by clement weather for most or all of your Camino. As I mentioned in the introduction to this section, both our Caminos were walked during spring months (April and May) and yet they could not have been more different.

Our first Camino was punctuated by extreme cold and wind in the Pyrenees that followed us as we descended into Rioja; a heat wave on the Meseta; snow in the Cantabrians, and endless days of rain in Galicia. In 2006, at almost exactly the same time of year, we had weeks of sunshine (even in Galicia!) and welcome cloud cover (but hardly any rain) across the Meseta. We even took gaiters for the snow we were expecting on this second walk, but the warm spring hit so suddenly that all the snow had melted and the gaiters were unnecessary.

The message is 'be prepared for anything!' so let's return to some more Camino preparation.

FITNESS: does it really matter?

There was an enormous difference between our first and second Caminos and it wasn't just the weather. We learned lots of hard lessons on our first Camino and physical preparation was one of the big ones.

There's no two ways about it – the fitter you are, the more enjoyable your Camino will be. It certainly is true that some people walk the Camino with little fitness or forethought. If you're the kind of person who enjoys relying on luck and you don't mind a surprise or two, then the 'get there and get started' approach might work – but it's not one I would personally recommend. For most of us who've done little regular, long-distance walking, some preparation and planning will make the road a lot easier.

Improving your cardio fitness (the kind that involves lifting your heart rate for a prolonged period of time) as well as your strength (through load-bearing exercise like weight training or walking with a pack) are essential in preparing to walk a Camino. For the less-fit, this means starting out slow and gradually working towards more walking, stair climbing, jogging or cycling – pretty much on a daily basis. This will improve your resting heart rate and your general level of fitness. In addition, you need to work at improving your 'staying power' by walking for longer and longer distances. The message is – start walking!

It's a good idea to get some professional guidance at a gym or fitness centre. You can get help with putting together an appropriate training program that will give you week-by-week targets leading up to your Camino. We also got advice on a series of simple stretches that we did each day on our Camino.

If you've got say, six to 12 months before you're going to walk the Camino, and you're not particularly fit, you can start with small steps and build up. Work out what your current idea of a 'decent walk' is (it might be twice around the block or it might be five kilometres) and start from there.

As you get closer to leaving for Spain, you should aim to clock up a regular 20 kilometres plus per day (preferably wearing the boots and the loaded pack you'll be using on the Camino).

As well as regular walking, yoga sessions were an important part of our preparation for both Caminos. For our second Camino we stepped it up a notch and practised basic yoga daily, as well as attending a couple of classes a week. A set of simple yoga stretches became part of our daily routine once we were in Spain.

Yoga, Pilates or any discipline that strengthens the core of your body as well as regularly stretching your muscles, is a useful part of your preparation for the Camino.

In the six months before we left, we attended yoga classes twice a week. The classes we chose also included instruction in the principles of the Alexander Technique. This technique encourages awareness and positive change when it comes to postural habits and the way we use our bodies. A couple of one-to-one sessions focusing on walking while carrying a pack and using walking poles while ascending, descending and flat-ground walking proved invaluable on the Camino.

Before our second Camino, we put together a simple set of stretches that we did at the beginning and end of every day. Once we were on the Camino, evening 'stretch time' became a sort of full stop to our walking day – it was a calm hiatus between the day's walk and the evening's rest. When we reached our accommodation for the night we'd shed our packs and boots and either lie on the floor (if there was room) or on our beds and take turns in 'leading' the 15-minute routine.

Just as with the weather, all this physical preparation for the Camino doesn't mean a predictable walk. Even if you've been walking pretty much daily in the weeks or months before you leave, there's really no way to prepare to walk almost 800 kilometres – except by walking almost 800 kilometres. So again, try not to set the bar too high in the first days of your Camino.

I still laugh at the spreadsheet Angela put together and that we confidently gave out to friends before we left. "If you want to know where we are on any given date – just look at the chart, that's where we'll be." It showed where we would be on every night of our five-week Camino and included a rest day every Sunday. We thought we had it all under control.

In many ways, it's true that "You don't walk the Camino, the Camino walks you."

On our first Camino we assumed that we would walk an average of 25 kilometres every day, beginning on Day 1. By the end of the first week we were already way behind our schedule – walking shorter distances than we'd planned and spending 'unallotted' time on 'non-scheduled activities' like stopping for coffee and a chat with other pilgrims, exploring beautiful villages, and picnicking for a second breakfast, lunch and afternoon tea (essential given the stunning countryside we were walking through). Our tendency to sleep in meant that often the pilgrims we'd meet on the path had started at least one village before us.

The planned 25 kilometres on Day 1 of our first Camino ended with us sitting down and refusing to get up again after about 12 kilometres!

BEST FOOT FORWARD: what to wear on your feet

Along with your pack, your boots are the most important thing you'll purchase. As you'll see when you visit an outdoor equipment specialist, there is an incredibly wide choice. Having made the decision to walk the Camino, buying the boots you're going to walk it in is pretty exciting. You'll probably be tempted to buy something on your first visit. Try not to rush. If you live in a city, there will be more than one outdoor gear specialist and each one will stock different brands of boots. It's a good idea to try a variety of them.

Choice of footwear is a very individual decision but there are a few broad guidelines that will help you. Although there are plenty of very steep hills on the Camino, there is no mountain climbing as such. You will always be on some kind of path, so very heavy mountain-climbing boots aren't necessary. What is crucial is that your boots give you adequate support, both underfoot and in stopping you from turning an ankle – much of the Camino is rocky, and an ancient Roman road, although incredibly beautiful, is less than easy to walk on!

Depending on your preference and on your knowledge of your own gait and walking tendencies, you might choose a shoe (the tough cross-country kind), a three-quarter boot or a full boot. I've seen all of these and more on the feet of pilgrims!

Stopping to adjust shoe laces

One thing that isn't a good idea is running shoes. They're just not tough enough and don't give enough support. Remember, you'll be walking over all kinds of terrain, including bitumen, dirt, mud and very rocky ground. You want footwear that will last the distance and protect your feet. In giving this advice, I'm assuming that you are planning to walk a fair distance on the Camino – not just a few days.

If you don't already have a favourite style of walking boot, this is where you need to start visiting outdoor equipment shops. Shop around a little until you find a shop and an assistant with whom you're comfortable. This means someone who'll take some time to get to know what you want your boots to do, and who'll take into account factors like the shape of your feet and the kind of socks you'll be wearing. You also want someone who isn't going to rush you and is happy for you to try on a range of boots. Many outdoor shops will allow you to purchase your boots, take them home and wear them around the house. If, after a few days you decide they're not right, you can take them back and exchange them.

Try on a few different styles and brands of boots and make sure you try them with the style of sock you'll be wearing on the Camino. There are a few 'Schools of Sock' when it comes to long-distance walking. Some insist on a sock liner (of cotton/wool or other blend) beneath a sock. Whatever your preference, the most important thing is that you change your socks at least once a day – heat and sweat are a recipe for blisters – so you'll need to take three pairs per person.

Make sure your boots have enough room around your toes and that your heel is held securely without being squeezed too tightly. Your heel should not move up and down in the boot as you walk. Many outdoor shops now stock moulded insoles that help to hold the heel firmly and provide support for the arch of the foot.

Remember that when you are walking, your feet will swell. With this in mind, if you are trying to choose between a boot that is slightly tight or slightly loose, go for the looser one. Also make sure that you can comfortably spread your toes while wearing your boots.

The next decision is whether to buy waterproof (usually 'Gore-Tex') boots or not. I wore non-waterproof boots on my first Camino and only regretted it in Galicia, where the rain was so insistent that I walked the final four days in boots that were little more than containers for rainwater. The main reason for this wasn't so much that my boots weren't 'Gore-Tex', but that my short pants meant that the rain ran down my legs and into the top of my boots. If you don't want to wear long, waterproof pants, gaiters are another option.

This is all a lot to take into account but buying the wrong boots can take up a lot more time and money. Angela bought an expensive pair of boots about eight months before we left for Spain. She discovered after a couple of months that they just weren't wearing-in correctly. They were still too tight around the toes. It was a big decision to buy a new pair of boots but it was probably one of the best decisions she made.

As well as your walking boots you'll need a second set of footwear to change into when you've finished walking at the end of each day. There's nothing better than pulling those boots off your hot, aching feet and changing into a pair of open sandals at the end of each day. Your feet really need that chance to breathe. If it's chilly, put your sandals on over a fresh pair of socks.

The most popular 'off the path' footwear are the style of sandal such as 'Teva' or 'Lizard' that still offer a modicum of support in their moulded sole as well as straps at front and back. Another advantage of this style of sandal is that, if you are suffering from blisters or sore feet, you can walk in them instead of your boots for a little while. While we took sandals like these on our first Camino, we chose to take 'Crocs' sandals on our second Camino. The main reason was that they are so much lighter while still being waterproof – a real advantage in communal showers.

OH MY ACHING FEET!
Foot care on the Camino

Apart from changing your socks regularly and giving your feet a rest in sandals every evening, here are a few more tips about looking after your feet on the Camino.

During your training for the Camino you may have noticed pain or tenderness in particular areas of your feet that have not eased over time. Good outdoor suppliers sell moulded inserts for boots that can make things much more comfortable.

If you think your foot problems are more serious and long-standing (pardon the pun), it's a good idea to get some professional advice. You may need orthotics, which are custom-made (and often expensive) inserts for your boots. It's important that you get this kind of advice as early as possible in your lead-up to the Camino as you will need to get used to the change these inserts create before you set out.

Blisters

Probably the most common foot problem on the Camino is blisters or 'ampollas'. I suspect that the economy of northern Spain is based on the sale of 'Compeeds' – a blister bandage sold in all the pharmacias along the Camino.

In 2006 I was really excited about spending a rest day in O'Cebreiro with its Celtic music and hearty Galician food. A nasty set of blisters meant that I'd be staying there whether I liked it or not:

> **Diary:** second Camino
>
> About 2km or so before O'Cebreiro the big blister on my heel burst. It lifted the skin up along the back of my heel as the fluid was pushed up by a particularly steep climb. The most awful feeling. I thought the blister patch had pulled off but it wasn't the patch, it was my skin! Yuck! Limped into O'Cebreiro and got a room in the 'overflow' building. A bit noisy and damp but I was just happy to be off my feet. Met up with H and M and had dinner at the nice taverna we remembered from 2004. Really friendly and great food. Woke up to stunning scenery – wonderful! The next day a steep climb straight up and out. My feet pretty painful but the mountain scenery was a good distraction.

How to prevent blisters? That's the million-dollar question. You'll come across lots of 'absolutely foolproof' theories about how to avoid blisters – they may work for some but not others.

Here are a few:

- Make sure you stay hydrated – not just while you're walking but also at night and before you start the day's walk. Dehydration is one of the causes of blisters
- As soon as you notice a 'hot spot' forming, dress it with a blister bandage or pad it with a wad of sheep's wool
- Keep your feet as cool and dry as possible. If your feet tend to sweat a lot, change into clean, dry socks a couple of times during the day
- 'Toughen' your feet by wiping them daily with methylated spirits.

If you do end up with blisters there are a couple of ways of dealing with them. The two methods outlined below, particularly the second, became part of our daily routine on the Camino because of my extraordinary gift for forming really bad blisters.

I got them on my first Camino (while walking across the hot, flat Meseta) and thought I'd learned my lessons about how to prevent them. I then managed to develop even more spectacularly deep specimens on my second Camino. So much for lessons learned.

Remember that the skin over a blister is dead, so it has no feeling. Just don't jab the tender flesh beneath.

- **Have a needle and thread and some disinfectant in your first aid kit. When a blister forms, pass the threaded, disinfected needle through one side of the blister and out the other and leave the thread in, so that it drains the fluid from the blister at either end.**
- **If you form very deep blisters (as opposed to shallow, surface ones), use sharp nail scissors (from your first aid kit) to cut a triangle-shaped hole (drainage point) in the blister near the edge. It won't hurt – it's just dead skin. It needs to be a fairly large hole so that the skin cannot heal over as you walk. Disinfect the scissors and the wound. Cover the wound with gauze and then bandage before walking. At bedtime, take the bandage off so the wound can 'air'. You will need to repeat this process at the beginning of each day until the blister heals. The blister will drain into the gauze, heal more quickly and be far less painful if it's not full of fluid.**

Shin splints

The most common, preventable problem we saw on the Camino was shin splints.

'Shin splint' is really a general term that covers a range of conditions. Basically it involves pain in the front of the lower leg due to anything from tight muscles and inflammation to a stress fracture. Most of the people we met on the Camino who were suffering from shin splints hadn't really done a lot of ongoing preparation for the Camino, or they'd ignored the early signs to rest.

Shin splints usually occur when your physical activity changes in some way – like upping the amount and intensity of walking you're doing – for example, when you start training for the

Camino. Noticing the problem while you are training is much better than encountering it on the Camino. You might need to stretch more thoroughly before and after you walk. You may also need to seek professional help from a physiotherapist or podiatrist.

If you are afflicted with shin splints on the Camino it's important not to just 'soldier on' as you can cause more problems. Take a bit of time out to apply 'RICE' – rest, ice, compression and elevation.

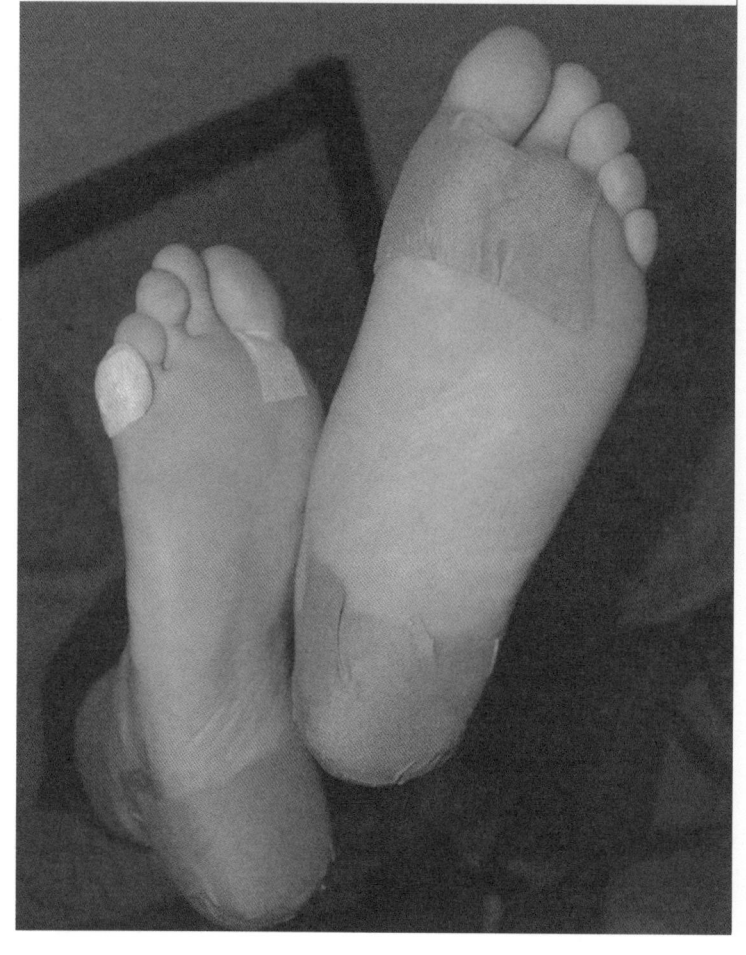

All bandaged up and ready to go

On our first Camino (left) our packs were bigger and heavier than on our second Camino (right)

KEEPING IT LIGHT: backpacks

The size of backpacks is measured in litres. The larger trekking packs are around 75 litres or more, which, in my hard-earned experience, is way too big for the Camino.

Aim for a 50-litre pack (some pilgrims manage 40 litres). The thing to remember is that if you take a big pack, you'll inevitably fill it!

Once you visit an outdoor equipment shop and have a look at a 50-litre pack, you'll see that it really isn't very big, but it's all you'll want to carry on the Camino. Bigger packs weigh more before you've even put anything in them. Remember, you don't need to carry a tent or cooking gear. You'll be staying in a pilgrims' refuge, a hotel or some other kind of accommodation each night, so you'll always have shelter and a bed.

Make sure that you choose a trekking pack, not a daypack. Trekking packs are designed around a good frame and an adjustable harness that will transfer most of the pack weight to your hips, while the shoulder and chest straps stabilise the load and pull it snugly across your back. You can also be fitted according to your body shape, with most good quality trekking packs available for torsos of different length. A daypack, with no frame or hip support to speak of, will pull on your shoulders and back. The difference between the two will become more obvious with every day that you walk!

Taking a smaller pack means that you're limited to absolute essentials. You should be aiming to carry around seven to ten kilograms. Some walkers swear by the rule of carrying that amount or no more than ten per cent of their body weight, whichever is lightest. This might not feel like much when you're just walking a few kilometres – but remember the 'accumulation factor' – every kilo gets heavier the further you walk.

When you think of going to the other side of the world and then walking for weeks through varying terrain and weather, you tend to want to pack a lot of things 'just in case'. Fight hard against this inclination. Practise saying to yourself in a confident tone "I can do without that". Otherwise, your feet, knees, hips and shoulders will be having a stern word with you on the Camino.

We carried 75-litre packs, full to the brim, on our first Camino. Once food and water were on board we were probably carrying around 15 kilograms. The second time around, our 50-litre packs held only the essentials and we got our loaded weight down to around 10 kilograms. I think that eight kilograms would be ideal.

Your pack should have a couple of external pockets or storage areas so that you can easily get to things like food or maps while you're walking. I think it's best to carry your water in a 'water bladder'. Most modern packs have a spot especially for it and an exit hole for the plastic tube. This means that your water tube sits in front of your shoulder and so encourages you to drink more often.

A waterproof pack liner makes a lot of sense given that the weather on the Camino is so unpredictable. Some walkers use plastic garbage bags but it's worth investing in a custom-made pack liner. They're unlikely to tear and they're certainly a lot less noisy when you're packing to leave a refugio at 6am.

We found it useful to separate our pack contents into a few different compression bags inside our packs. Our backpacks were completely emptied and then repacked each morning and evening on the Camino. With the possible exception of wet weather gear, we used every single thing in our packs each day. Rather than having everything in one big jumble, it helps to know which bag contains what. Compression bags also do what their name suggests – compress your pack contents into smaller bundles. There are plenty of different brands of these bags in outdoor equipment shops.

It's useful to take a small, lightweight pouch, pack or bumbag for the evenings when you need to carry your passport, money, camera and other valuables. We bought a tiny (and cheap) day pack that was just big enough for our essentials.

We chose a camera bag that could be threaded onto the front hip belt of the backpack. That way, the camera was readily at hand and its weight was not adding to the backpack.

KEEPING IT LIGHTER STILL:
clothes and kit

We received some great advice from a knowledgeable salesperson in our favourite outdoor gear shop. He talked us through the principles behind 'dressing in layers'. It reminded me of when I used to do a bit of cross-country skiing and wore clothes that I could pile on or strip off as heat or cold dictated. It makes sense that the same goes for long-distance walking.

As with backpacks, lightweight clothes make a big difference to the weight your body has to carry. The answer for us was fine-spun merino wool garments. Except for our underwear, trousers and jackets, all of our clothes were made of different grades of fine-spun wool. The wool is so fine that it doesn't feel like wool. Most importantly, it doesn't itch at all! As well as being incredibly lightweight, these clothes are made to wick moisture away from your body so that it can evaporate more easily. They also dry really quickly after being washed. There are a number of brands making these products now so there is a wide choice as well as more opportunity to catch items on sale.

One of the many things we really appreciated about the fine, pure wool clothes was the fact that they can go quite a while between washes – they don't smell. A mighty advantage on the Camino!

Fine wool outdoor clothes follow a grading system relating to layers: skin, mid and outer layers. In the list of pack contents below, the fine wool garments are marked with a (w):

PACK CONTENTS

We each took:

CLOTHES

- Underwear (include a pair of 'Skins' shorts if you are prone to chafing on your upper thighs)
- socks x 3
- thermal singlet (w) x 2
- thermal long sleeve (w) x 2
- long johns (w) x 1
- pants/shorts x 2
- T-shirt (w) x 2
- lightweight windbreaker jacket or vest
- wet weather gear (pants & jacket or poncho)
- feather down jacket
- beanie
- lightweight gloves
- tube-shaped neckerchief that can also be used as a bandana
- lightweight sun hat with good cover
- sunglasses
- sandals or 'Crocs'
- 2 stuff bags for clothes – 1 for wet weather gear only.

Some might question the need for a down-filled jacket as well as a windbreaker jacket. We found, on both Caminos, that we needed the windbreaker for cold walking days. Almost every night we wore our down jackets after we'd showered and changed and headed out for a walk and dinner. Particularly outside the summer months, nights on the Camino can be quite chilly and sometimes really cold. Bodies that have been exerting themselves all day also tend to cool down quickly and it's good to be able to slip into a light but very warm jacket.

The 'skin layer' singlets and long johns were great for really cold weather and also doubled as pyjamas. The rest of our kit was made up of:

SLEEPING:
- **lightweight sleeping bag** (a warmer one if you're planning on staying in refugios. Even if you're going to stay in private accommodation, take a lightweight sleeping bag just in case.)
- **pillowcase** (If you're staying in refugios, some of the pillows may not be all that clean. The other option is to use a T-shirt as a pillow case.)

TOILETRIES:
- toothbrush/paste/floss
- skin sunscreen and moisturiser
- lip balm sunscreen
- body wash/shampoo
- tweezers
- nail clippers/file
- toilet paper/tissues
- small trowel and bags for sanitary disposal
- baby/personal wipes.

MISCELLANEOUS:
- guide book
- Spanish phrase book
- pen/paper/journal
- camera
- **mobile phone** (for emergencies, booking accommodation, staying in touch with other pilgrims)
- phone charger
- power plug adapter
- travel wallet
- lightweight bowl/mug/cutlery
- small rope
- small torch
- small whistle (to attract attention if needed)
- Swiss Army knife

- **towel** (lightweight microfibre)
- **'Sard' soap** (for clothes washing)
- **nappy pins** (for hanging clothes on line or back of pack)
- **needle and thread**
- **handkerchief** (men's size – always useful)
- **plastic bags** (sealable).

FIRST AID:
- basic bandages/band aids
- iodine or other disinfectant
- pawpaw ointment or similar
- ear plugs
- **blister bandages** (easily found in pharmacias along the Camino)
- cotton buds/wool
- 'Panadol'/aspirin
- anti-inflammatory gel
- arnica cream
- tinea cream
- eye drops.

NUTRITION: (see page 90 for more on this)
- nutrition supplements
- **hydration powder** (e.g. 'Gastrolyte' tablets)
- protein powder
- **nutrition powder** (e.g. 'Vital Greens').

HYDRATION:
- **Water bladder.** As mentioned earlier, most packs have a special spot for the water bladder. It's better than a bottle because the mouthpiece sits on the front strap of your pack, making it easier to drink often. To find out how to maintain and clean your water bladder make sure you read the instructions that come with it.

Walking with '4 legs' is much easier on the body.

WALKING POLES:
an extra pair of legs

When I first started planning for the Camino I must admit I had a pretty romantic image of myself as a pilgrim – carrying one simple wooden staff, perhaps fashioned from a Spanish tree branch – just like those in the paintings and statues of the pilgrims of old.

On one of our many preparatory visits to the outdoor shops in Little Bourke Street, Melbourne, a young sales assistant gave us the lowdown on the more modern version of the pilgrim staff – the adjustable, telescopic, granite-tipped walking pole. He reeled off the statistics about the percentage of load they take off your knees and hips while walking, and he described their ability to act as a second set of legs when on steep ascents and descents.

Our sales assistant urged us to buy two each, pointing out that when carrying a pack (particularly on steep descents) we are top-heavy animals and benefit most from a solid base of four legs to lean on. He ended up convincing us and I owe him a debt of gratitude. Thanks to him, neither of us had a fall on the Camino, though we witnessed a few nasty ones – usually on steep descents.

While on the first few days we felt a little silly walking along with a pole in each hand, they soon became an extension of our bodies and we only put them away when we were walking through the larger towns and cities. As well as proving invaluable through the hills and mountains, they made the long flat sections so much easier, helping us to maintain an even walking rhythm and beating a gentle time with their tap, tap, tap.

Another plus gained from walking poles is that they prevent 'sausage fingers' – swollen fingers and hands that result from poor upper-body circulation. Some walkers also get 'pins and needles' in their arms and/or hands. By using walking poles you'll be exercising all of your body, not just your legs. You'll find that circulation in your upper body will increase. A bonus is that muscle tone in your arms and shoulders will improve along with your calves!

FUEL TO BURN: food on the Camino

It pretty much goes without saying that the food you put into your body over a long-distance trek like the Camino is incredibly important. Like most of our other big Camino lessons, we learned this lesson the hard way on our first Camino when we made the mistake of allowing our bodies to dictate when and what we ate. That might sound like a sensible thing to do in ordinary circumstances but walking around 25 kilometres a day for weeks on end isn't really 'normal circumstances.' We found that our bodies sent out curiouser and curiouser messages as the days and weeks went by.

One of the most obvious of these strange messages was a tendency to not feel hunger in the same way I usually would. Instead, at around 3pm, my stomach would feel as though it

Sneaking in a treat

was twisting into a bit of a knot. It didn't make me feel like eating, it just felt uncomfortable. I eventually worked out that this was my body's new interpretation of feeling hungry.

Angela reported having the same experience. Hot on the tail of this twisty knot-in-the-stomach feeling would be a pretty dramatic dip in energy often accompanied by one or both of us getting a tad grumpy.

On our first Camino, our answer to this sudden physical mayday was to eat the best part of a block of chocolate and a bag of crisps. Meltdown would be averted for an hour or so but then the arrow on the energy dial would swing back to zero, usually just as we were walking the final kilometres to our destination for the day.

That meant that we'd arrive in towns and villages with hardly enough energy to do our stretches, basic washing, shower and change. Let alone go for a walk to explore the town before dinner.

A Slow Walk Across Spain

Between our first and second Caminos we worked out that a big part of our exhaustion at the end of each day was due to the kind of food we were eating and when we were eating it.

After a bit of research, we came up with a different eating plan for our second Camino. It involved eating more often throughout the day and cutting way down on processed food like crisps and chocolate. That also meant limiting the amount of sugar we ate. Of course, we had the odd chocolate treat but it was no longer a part of our daily diet.

The difference in our energy levels and endurance was extraordinary. There was hardly a day on our second Camino when we didn't go for a walk after arriving in the village or town where we were going to spend the night. We actually had energy to spare.

Angela also did some research on food supplements and into our packs went protein powder and a vitamin/mineral supplement. There's not a steady supply of vegetables (particularly green ones) on the Camino, so to make up for that we mixed a scoop of 'Vital Greens' into our orange juice each morning.

In the afternoons, before the energy level had a chance to drop, we'd have a scoop of protein powder (a quarter of the recommended dose) mixed into a small bottle of water. Not as tasty as chocolate but way more sustaining. Although we often didn't feel like taking either supplement, we'd learned not to always trust what our body was saying and we stuck to our regime. The same went for staying hydrated. We didn't just drink when we were thirsty but prompted each other to drink every 15 minutes while walking and also to drink plenty of water at night and in the mornings.

> **ORGANISING SUPPLEMENTS**
> We took two large plastic containers of powdered supplements with us. When we got to the south of France we spent our first jet-lagged night measuring batches of each supplement into snap-lock bags. We measured enough to last us from the Pyrenees to Leon and posted the rest to ourselves at Leon Post Office. The CSJ guidebook yellow pages will tell you how to do this.

In Spain, breakfast is often fairly insubstantial.

THE BEAT OF A DIFFERENT DRUM: Spanish meal times vs. Camino meal times

Like most countries, Spain marks each section of its day with a meal. It goes pretty much like this:

7-9am: 'el desayuno' or breakfast
10am-noon: 'tapas' or little meals
1.30-3pm: 'la comida' or lunch (the main meal of the day)
3-4.30pm: siesta time
4.30-5pm: 'la merienda' or snack
9pm-midnight: 'la cena' or dinner

Generally speaking, those meal and rest times don't fit in with the food and rest needs of pilgrims walking the Camino. For example, our meals were typically:

7-9am: breakfast (coffee, orange juice, vegetable supplement powder, toast and jam)
10.30am: morning tea (fresh fruit, bread & cheese, nuts)
Noon: lunch (tuna baguette, fruit)
2.30pm: afternoon tea (protein supplement, fruit, nuts)
7.30pm: dinner (three courses, see 'pilgrim menu' on page 93)

At least breakfast time coincided with our Spanish environment. However, for most Spanish people breakfast is just a quick nod to the beginning of their day. They're still running on the fuel of the meal they had late the previous night. A typical Spanish breakfast is 'café con leche' or coffee with milk, freshly squeezed orange juice and a piece of cake or the Spanish equivalent to fried doughnuts – 'churros.' It's pretty much caffeine and sugar. For many of the older men who arrive early in the bars, a shot of the local firewater and a cigarette are also part of breakfast.

For pilgrims, this can be a bit difficult as a decent breakfast is vital. If you're staying in a refugio that has cooking facilities then breakfast can be planned and prepared. Some private accommodation caters to pilgrims and overseas tourists and offers more substantial breakfasts. However, because we often stayed in rooms above bars, where breakfast usually meant a few small pieces of toasted white bread and some jam in those little plastic packs, we would shop the night before so that we could have our 'second breakfast' or morning tea fairly early.

If the weather was inclement and we happened to be in a village or town at lunchtime we'd head to a bar for 'tapas' instead of having our usual picnic lunch. A bar lunch meant the ever-present 'bocadillo', a bread roll with a filling such as omelette ('tortilla') or ham and cheese. A bocadillo, given that it's carbs and protein, is good fuel at the midway point of the day.

Our top 10 gastronomic experiences on the Camino included meals in bars and hostals but quite a few of the top spots on the list were taken by particularly memorable lunchtime picnics.

Picnics were pretty much a daily occurrence, weather permitting. The level of memorableness was more about the location than what we were eating – that never really changed. Lunch was almost always one baguette cut in half, a tin of tuna each, a couple of triangles of 'Laughing Cow' cheese and, if we could get it, some lettuce and freshly squeezed lemon. We'd have an orange or a banana for dessert and wash it all down with water. Favourite locations were clearings in shady woods, outcrops with stunning views into the distance, or large objects such as rocks or ruins that provided a shield from the elements.

Picnics were a daily highlight.

The evening meal was a daily highlight because it meant not only that we were showered and wearing comfy sandals, but we also got a long sit down, a hot meal and a bottle of the local red shared with new friends.

The villages along the Camino have been hosting pilgrims for centuries and they have worked out that if pilgrims have to wait for the Spanish dinnertime they'll be asleep at the table. Most bars along the Camino offer a Pilgrim Menu del Dia at around 7.30pm. It adds to the daily sense of routine by being one of the most predictable things on the Camino.

This is a typical pilgrim menu:
- **Primer Plato (first course):** salad (usually with white asparagus), pasta or soup
- **Segundo Plato (second course):** a thin piece of pan-fried meat (usually pork or beef), home-cut chips and grilled red capsicum. Every now and again there will be fish (local trout if you're lucky) or chicken
- **Postre (dessert):** 'flan' (crème caramel), yoghurt (or related dairy products) with sugar or honey, or a piece of fresh fruit
- Wine or water
- Bread.

There are regional variations, such as the wonderful potato soup in Galicia. Of course, you can choose to eat in restaurants in the bigger towns if you can wait until they open. We tended to go to restaurants on the night before a rest day, knowing we could stay up late.

"THERE'S ONLY A BIT OF HAM IN IT": vegetarians on the Camino

The Spanish diet can be tricky to negotiate for vegetarians. The Spanish love their meat. In almost every town there are whole shops devoted to 'jamón' (ham). Cutting out meat will make what is already a fairly limited menu pretty sparse. Pescatarians (those who eat fish) have a slightly easier time of it, as tuna and other fish are fairly common on pilgrim menus. For example, many salads and pasta dishes contain tuna.

The options for vegetarians are salad with no tuna, pasta with no tuna, fried eggs and chips (most bars will make this if requested), tortilla, and plenty of bread and cheese. If you're staying in a refugio (with a kitchen), then it's easier to shop and cook your own meals.

Whole shops are devoted to 'jamón' (ham).

I received an email recently from one of our workshop participants who'd just walked the Camino. She is vegetarian and reported that there are more and more vegetarian options on pilgrim menus.

If you have very specific dietary requirements then it's crucial that you learn how to say them in Spanish, so keep the phrasebook handy when you go out for a meal.

Don't judge an albergue by first appearances.

ACCOMMODATION: it takes all kinds

Accommodation can be one of the points of contention among pilgrims on the Camino. Do 'real' pilgrims stay in private accommodation or are they copping out? Does the spirit of pilgrimage demand that you cast off all material luxury, including your own room and shower? You'll be sure to jump into this discussion a few times during the walk.

There were times when Angela and I received some distinctly judgemental looks from some holier-than-us pilgrims because we mostly chose to stay in private accommodation. Yet there were always plenty of other pilgrims in the bars and hostals where we stayed.

Broadly speaking, accommodation options on the Camino can be divided into two categories – communal or private. Each has its advantages and disadvantages and, of course, its advocates and detractors.

A Slow Walk Across Spain

Communal accommodation options on the Camino are known as 'refugios' or 'albergues' (both are words for the same thing – accommodation that's similar to a youth hostel) and most carry on the centuries-old tradition of offering pilgrims cheap or (increasingly rare) free accommodation.

Originally, many of these refugios were run by orders of monks such as the Benedictines or the Monks of Cluny. Most of them administered to the medical and nutritional as well as the spiritual needs of pilgrims – some even offered clothes and shoe-mending services, even a haircut!

Today, almost every village, town and city has at least one refugio and the standard of accommodation on offer is as varied as the refugios are plentiful. In more recent years there are more 'private refugios' appearing – particularly in Galicia. These refugios tend to be a little more expensive. They may have twin rooms available, as well as a few extra amenities.

Refugios provide anything from the most basic accommodation – a bed (usually a bunk) and access to water (not always hot) – to the almost luxurious – a bed, blanket, pillow, meal (or a kitchen to prepare one in), hot water, clothes washers and dryers,

LEFT: A very nice albergue in Boadilla del Camino
BELOW: A typical room above a bar

heating and even some Gregorian chanting! Refugios will all fall somewhere between these two extremes.

Rooms or dormitories in refugios hold anything from five to 100 pilgrims (dorms and some bathrooms are mixed – not separate for male and female). You can expect to be woken as early as 6am as the 'hospitaleros' (wardens) have to clean and prepare for the next night's group of pilgrims.

At the busiest times of the year, there can be a tendency for pilgrims to start rushing to the next refugio in order to secure a bed (doors usually open around 2pm). Try not to get caught up in this kind of race. Even if you are walking in the busiest months of July and August, there is always somewhere to stay, even if it means a local offering you a room!

Staying in a refugio you can expect to share stories and conversation with pilgrims from all over the world and if there is a communal kitchen facility, meal times can be a highlight.

Most towns and villages along the Camino offer a choice of private or communal accommodation. There are a wide range of options that come under the 'private' category, and like the refugios, standards can vary enormously.

Diary: first Camino

In the early days of our walk, we stayed in a refugio that had only just been built. It was run as a family enterprise and mother and daughter ushered us into a fire-warmed common room. Dinner (cheap at five euros extra) was a three-course meal of salad, fried pork with grilled red capsicum and hot chips, and a dessert of fresh fruit. Sharing the meal was a Dutch woman, Anna, who was enjoying her long service leave solo on the Camino. There was also Maurice from Belgium, who, when we complained of aching feet, rummaged in his backpack and produced a fragrant balm that he'd made himself. "It will cure any kind of muscle problem", he claimed as he grabbed Angela's foot and started rubbing. "It's made from the wildflowers of my country!" I waited patiently for my turn.

Cost doesn't always reflect quality but generally speaking, the hotels (or 'hostals'), rural houses ('casas rurales') and rooms above bars and taverns offer accommodation that is clean and comfortable and that ranges from basic to downright luxurious. The cheapest and most plentiful private option is a room above a bar.

The obvious advantages of staying in private accommodation include (usually) hot water, a comfortable bed, clean linen and a break from snorers (unless, of course, you're sharing your room with one – I take this opportunity to thank Angela for her forbearance).

Guides to the Camino always list at least some private accommodation along with the refugios and usually include phone numbers in case you want to book ahead. Booking ahead isn't necessary unless it's a very busy time of year (the Easter week, or 'Semana Santa', for example), or you are walking the final 100 kilometres leading into Santiago. The number of pilgrims increases dramatically there and accommodation can be scarce. We always booked ahead to make sure of a room.

YOUR BED ON YOUR BACK:
camping on the Camino

On our first Camino, Angela and I took a small tent and sleeping mats. We carried this extra weight for two and a half weeks before realising that we didn't need (or want) them. Posting them on to ourselves in Santiago felt better than cleaning out the spare room!

Some people do carry a tent on the Camino but unless you have a total aversion to staying within cooee of another human, my advice is to leave it at home. There are not a lot of camping grounds along the Camino so you'll either need to set up your tent in woods or fields or ask to put it up in the grounds of a refugio.

If you are still keen to camp, join one of the pilgrim forums on the internet and ask questions of other pilgrims who have camped along the Camino.

MEADOW STOPS:
toilets on the Camino

The Camino doesn't 'do' public toilets.

The closest thing would be the restroom in a public bar (one of the few places where the Spanish aren't particularly house-proud).

Given that there are usually quite a few kilometres between towns and villages on the Camino, it's inevitable that one will be caught needing to do No.1s or No.2s (!) in the middle of a field, forest or mountain pass. Don't recoil but instead, adopt the scouts' motto: 'Be prepared!'

Carrying toilet paper is obviously a given. A packet of baby wipes (they even smell like soap) can add a bit of luxury to your 'meadow stop.' The other advantage of using personal or baby wipes as well as toilet paper is that you'll go a long way to preventing that arch enemy of the pilgrim – chafing.

When the call of nature becomes too insistent to ignore, you'll start scanning the surrounding landscape for a screened area like a clump of trees, a rocky outcrop or, in desperate circumstances, a small shrub. Just remember that there are lots of pilgrims on the Camino and many of them will have spotted the same landmark with similar relief, so watch where you walk.

For obvious reasons, carry a small trowel with you and some plastic bags so that you can take any sanitary objects to be disposed of in the next village (unfortunately, you'll probably be surprised at the number of people who haven't done the same).

"SAVE YOURSELF!"
Safety on the Camino

People who attend our workshops often ask about safety on the Camino. One common fear is that of dogs. Personally, I think it has become a little over-exaggerated, but let's separate fear and reality.

Firstly, there are lots of dogs along the Camino. Most are not going to bother you because they are either chained or caged (which means they are working/hunting dogs), are under the watchful eye of a shepherd or are tucked snugly under the arm of their city owner.

There is one breed of dog that deserves your respect in the form of giving it a wide berth. The maremma sheepdog is an ancient breed that is used to protect herds of sheep from predators such as wolves. They are able to protect a flock of sheep on their own, without a shepherd.

Angela and I met a maremma and its flock on our second Camino and it made its intentions clear by walking slowly towards us in a very no-nonsense way. We obligingly ducked under a fence and cut across an adjacent field. It added a kilometre or two to our day's walk but was the sensible thing to do.

The only other run-ins we had with dogs on the Camino were when I had to fend off a Jack Russell that wanted a piece of my heel (I used a baguette I'd just bought) and during an incident we call 'The Running of the Cows.'

Pilgrims often share the path with cows, particularly in Galicia. Herds are moved from place to place along the narrow roads, usually with a shepherd or two and their trusty dogs. Just stand to one side, let them go by and all should go well. Now and again, however, there will be an exception to the norm:

ABOVE: The path is sometimes shared with different pilgrims.

LEFT: Angela makes a friend.

Diary: second Camino

Yesterday we were walking through beautiful country on a narrow dirt road that wound around the sides of thickly wooded hills. Looking back we could see across three or four bends of the road behind us and we caught glimpses of a herd of cows being driven along by the usual husband and wife farming team. Angela has always been nervous about cows and was starting to get a bit edgy. "Don't worry", I reassured her, "they won't come this far", I couldn't resist stirring her and every now and then I'd stop and listen and whisper, "I think I can hear their hooves", But next thing, the farmer came flying around the corner, 30 horned cows in hot pursuit. It was the 'Running of the Cows' and we were trapped. The farmer saw us

A Slow Walk Across Spain

and expertly skidded sideways as he tried to stop the bovine charge. He was successful with the centre of the herd but those around the edges galloped past him, startled now and heading straight for us. I shouted to Angela to get off the path and pulled her up to a spot next to a gate, not realising that was the gate that the farmer and the cows were headed for. So farmer, wife, 30 cows and 2 dogs charged straight at us with Angela yelling, "Run! Run! Save yourself!" (it's nice to know that she's there for me in a crisis) and me yelling, "No! Don't run!" The smallest of the dogs decided at that point that I was a threat to its herd and went me like a rabid bathmat. As I tried to fend it off with my walking poles, the farmer directed the cows with a deafening example of the local language, and his wife yelled at the tiny terrier to leave me alone. It wouldn't, so she picked up a stick and, with practised expertise, sent it spinning fast to the dog's backside (an impressively small target). The dog yelped and ran back to the herd, the gate to the paddock was shut behind the cows and Angela stopped running and started to catch her breath. We said a heartfelt and breathless "muchos gracias" to the woman. She replied in a characteristic Galician deadpan, "De nada." ("It's nothing").

Other than this, our interactions with canines and other animals on the Camino were characterised by mutual curiosity and affection.

Walking alone

We met lots of people of all ages walking the Camino alone. Many of them were women. Although you can never totally guarantee that you'll be safe anywhere, I think the Camino Francés is one of the safest solo walks. This is partly because of the tendency for pilgrims to look out for each other but also due to the palpable sense of awareness amongst most pilgrims that they are sharing a significant journey.

Nevertheless, it's still important to take basic precautions. We always kept money and passports with us. In cities and large towns, particularly in crowded places, pickpockets are as skilled as anywhere in the world. It's not a good idea to carry a wallet in a back pocket for example. Just apply the traveller's basic common sense.

Other pilgrims form an invaluable network of support on the Camino – whether it's offering to bandage a blister, or taking time to talk when someone is doing it tough. There is an unspoken rule that pilgrims are there for each other. For me, this added to the sense of safety I felt.

PILGRIM ETIQUETTE:
the Spirit of the Camino

The Camino traverses private and public land and passes through many villages and towns. Although it is true that the people of northern Spain benefit from the Camino in terms of the 'tourism' it brings, they also have to host the constant stream of pilgrims that flows past their door. Many locals, particularly the older ones, show a great deal of respect for pilgrims and most pilgrims reciprocate.

I don't think we ever encountered local people who were rude or unwelcoming. In some of the villages, the locals can seem a bit gruff but we realised after a while that this is a cultural difference. A simple "Buenos dias" (good day) is usually the greeting in bars in Spain. When it came to the old men in the local bars, it was just a deep-throated "Diiaaaaass". Years of smoking have turned their voices into baritones! We found that the Spanish do not tend to be demonstrative at first – but with a

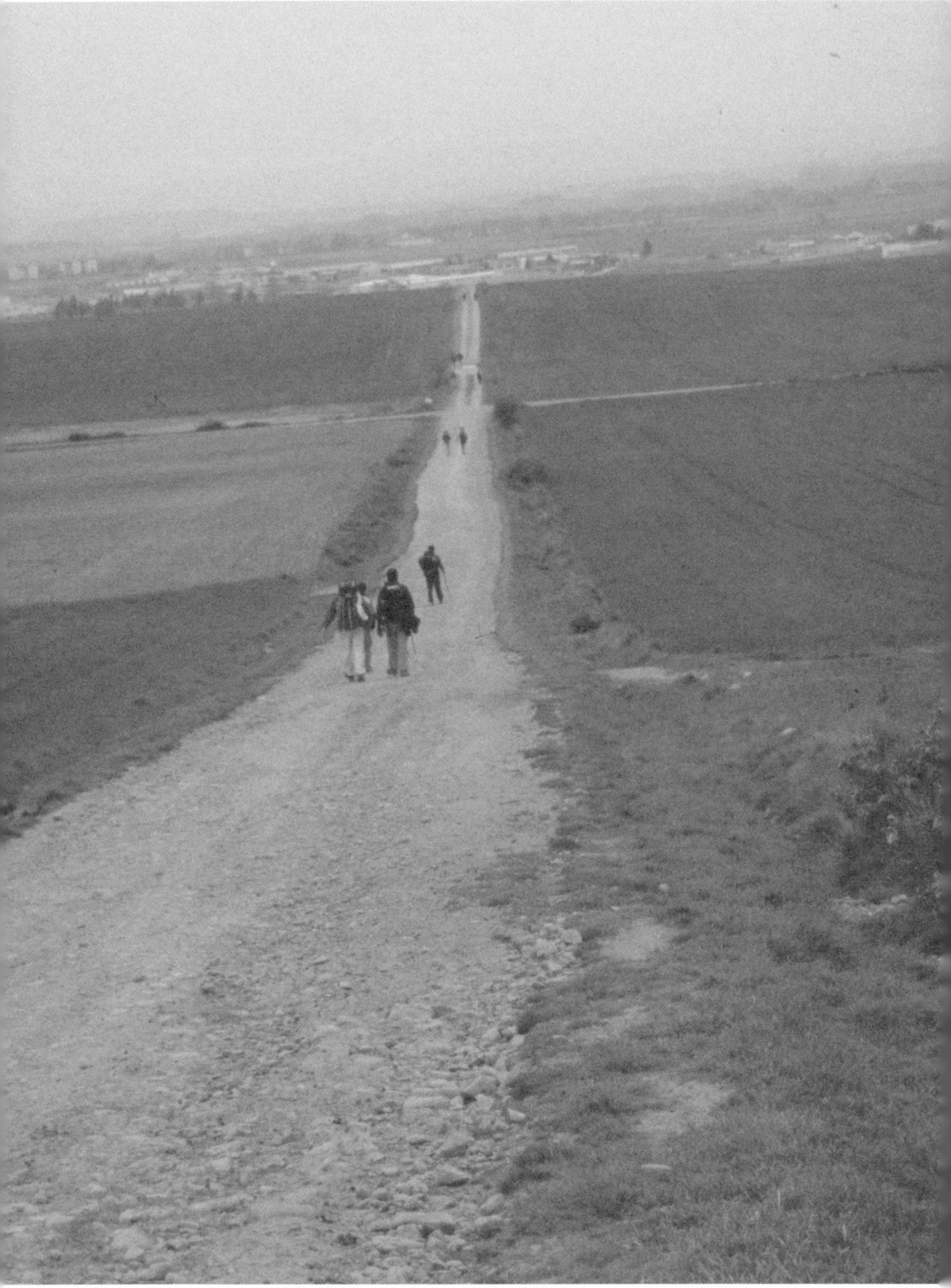

LEFT: Pilgrim traffic on the Camino

little patience on our part their warm-heartedness and humour inevitably shone through.

On our first Camino we had a lovely encounter with a bus load of elderly Spaniards:

Diary: first Camino

Walking along the pilgrim path beside a four-lane highway. Across the highway was a parked tour bus full of elderly Spaniards peering at us through each window in a line of excited faces. It seemed like a big deal to them to encounter pilgrims. Perhaps they were from another region. They were waving at us, so we waved back, thinking that would be the end of it. But then the tour guide, who spoke some English, got out of the bus and enthusiastically beckoned us over. I sent Angela as our ambassador. She was quite ceremoniously presented with a plastic bag full of 'goodies' that were clearly donations from the elderly tourists. When Angela came back across the highway and gave me the bag there was more excited waving and calling of "Buen Camino" as the bus drove off. Upon examining the contents of this gift we found one bottle of water, one pear, one home-made ham and cheese bocadillo wrapped in foil, and at the bottom, a half-chewed crust of bread. It made our day.

A Slow Walk Across Spain

People dig deep (both physically and mentally) on the Camino, and it can mean we tread a thin line when it comes to our ability to tolerate each other's peculiarities. We might have enjoyed walking and talking with a person but then realise that we need some time to walk alone for a bit. It's not uncommon for people to say that they want some time out – or simply to spend a little longer at a rest stop so that others can go on ahead. Whether you're walking with someone you know or someone you've recently met, it's important to be able to take (or give) time to be alone when it's needed.

When it comes to other pilgrims, particularly if you are staying in refugios, you will have plenty of opportunities to practise patience and generosity. There's no better place to be reminded of how different we all are than on the Camino. There will be people you are drawn to, who you'll want to walk and talk with, and there will be others who you will want to avoid at every opportunity.

Reading this section on the practicalities of walking a Camino has surely left you with an appetite – or at least the inclination to do something practical. Here are a couple of main course Spanish recipes to get you working out in the kitchen.

A popular rest stop

Trout with jamón
Serves 4

INGREDIENTS
4 whole trout
8 thin slices of jamón serrano (or prosciutto)
plain flour to dust
olive oil for frying
lemon wedges

METHOD
Rinse fish and pat dry.
Season fish with salt and pepper and add two slices of jamón in the belly of each fish.
Dust with flour and set aside.
Heat olive oil in frypan and fry the fish until golden on each side.
Serve with lemon wedges.

Potato tortilla
Serves 4

INGREDIENTS
6 eggs
1kg potatoes, peeled and thinly sliced
100ml extra virgin olive oil
Salt & pepper

METHOD
Heat oil in a heavy-based frypan (20cm diameter), add the potatoes and season with salt.

Gently cook, turning once until potatoes have softened (about 15 minutes).

Remove from heat, drain any excess oil and place the potatoes in a bowl. Lightly beat eggs with some salt and pepper and add to the potatoes. Mix well.

Return the pan to the heat and add a drizzle of the oil. Add the potato and egg mixture and gently cook until the base of the omelette has set.

To flip the omelette, take a plate that is a bit larger than the frypan, and place on top. With a quick motion, tip the omelette onto the plate and then slide it back into the pan, so that it is now flipped in the frypan.

Cook for a few more minutes and serve.

Bodegas Irache
desde 1891

FUENTE DE VINO
Bodegas Irache S.L.

**PROHIBIDO BEBER VINO
A MENORES DE 18 AÑOS**

LEY FORAL 10/1991 DE 16 DE MARZO
SOBRE PREVENCION Y LIMITACION
DEL CONSUMO DE BEBIDAS ALCOHOLICAS
POR MENORES DE EDAD.

La Casa del Bacalao (the House of Salted Cod) in Estella

Whole bars are devoted to Pulpo (octopus) in Galicia.

Tapas is always a treat, as in this bar in Puente la Reina.

Rioja vineyards in early Spring

A Basque house in the Pyrenees

'A 'palloza' in O'Cebeiro, Galicia

All made of stone

A beautiful Romanesque church

Saint James in the ancient chapel in Roncesvalles

Mourning procession, Easter Thursday, Burgos

Monks prepare to hoist the Botafumeiro (a giant incense censor) before swinging it across the heads of the congregation, Santiago de Compostela.

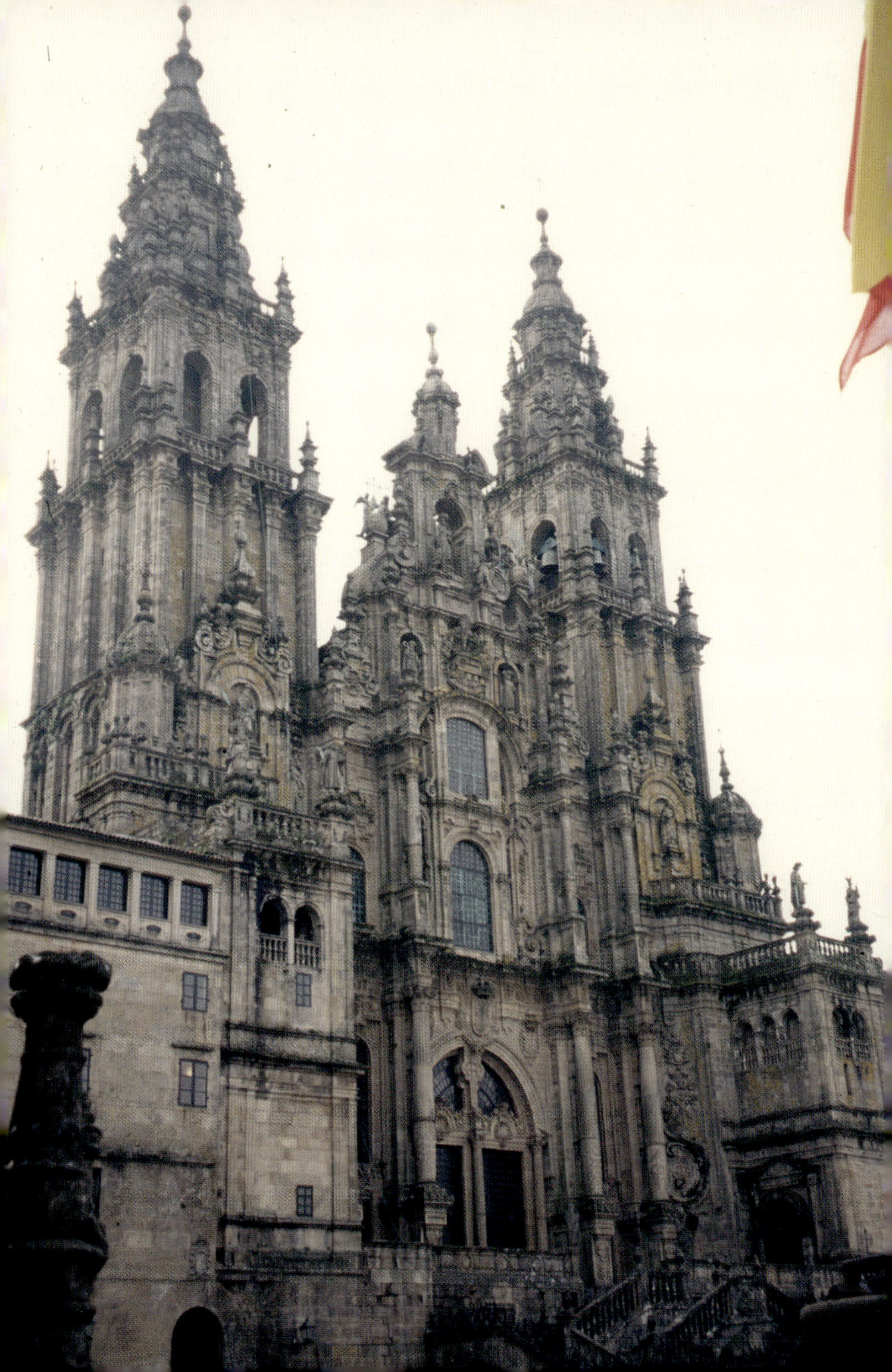

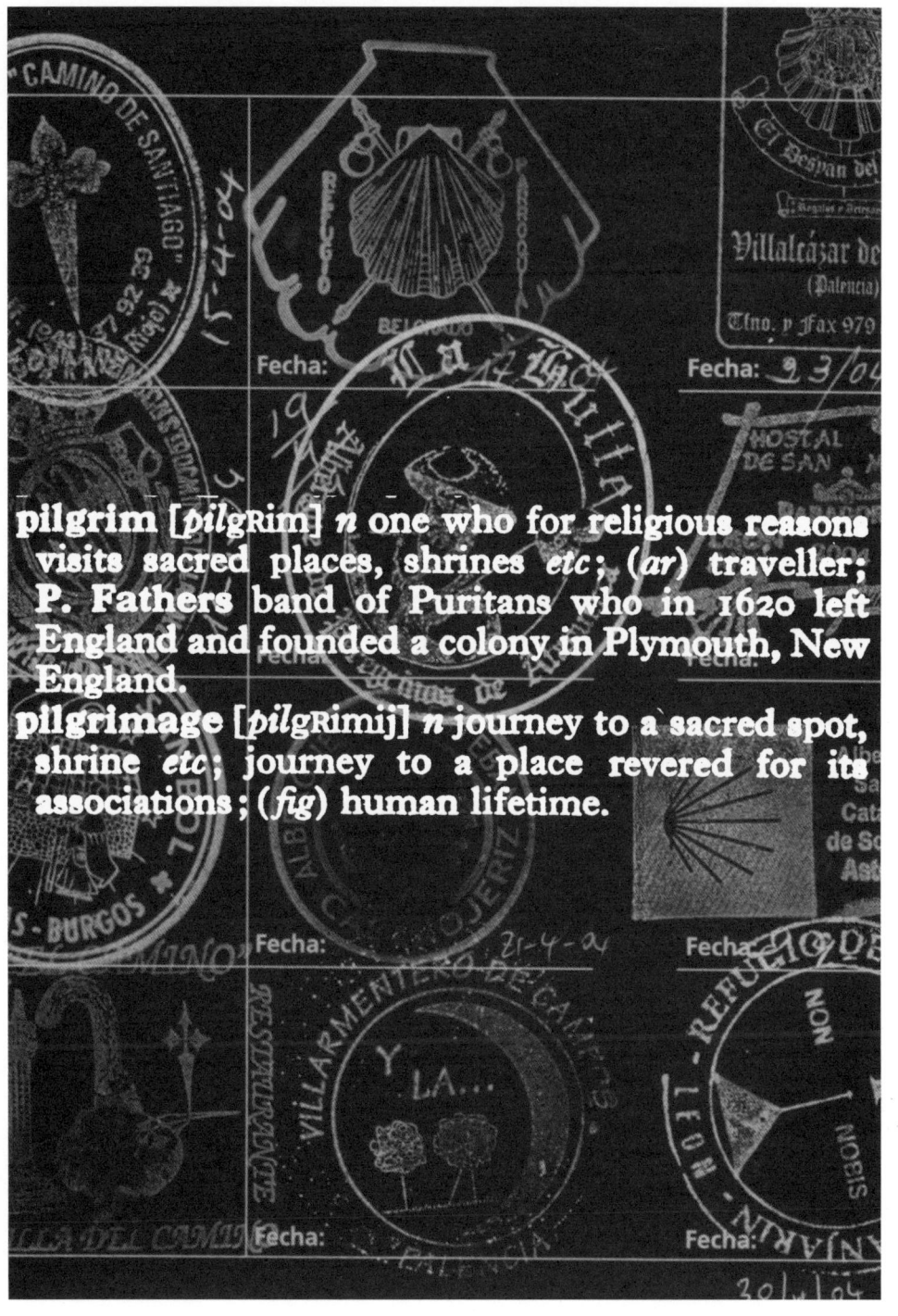

pilgrim [*pil*GRim] *n* one who for religious reasons visits sacred places, shrines *etc*; (*ar*) traveller; **P. Fathers** band of Puritans who in 1620 left England and founded a colony in Plymouth, New England.
pilgrimage [*pil*GRimij] *n* journey to a sacred spot, shrine *etc*; journey to a place revered for its associations; (*fig*) human lifetime.

03

Pilgrim sculptures
outside Pamplona

THE HISTORY OF THE CAMINO

THE HISTORY OF THE CAMINO

The incredible narrative that is the history of the Camino de Santiago has a cast of characters that originates in every part of the Iberian Peninsula (what we now call Spain and Portugal) and beyond. It is a history that spans religion and race – Christian, Islamic, Jewish, Celtic, Basque, Roman, Goth and Berber – and is reflected in the many names by which the peninsula and its regions have been known (Hispania, Asturias, Al-Andalus, to name a few).

Ancient ruins on the Camino

03 THE HISTORY OF THE CAMINO

ALL ROADS LEAD TO SANTIAGO:
the many Ways of Saint James

Many know the Camino de Santiago as the Way of Saint James. However, it's not so well known that there are many historic pilgrimage routes to Santiago. In medieval times, these various Caminos or 'ways' originated in Italy, France, Belgium, England, Scandinavia, Portugal and the different regions of Spain – in fact, from wherever a pilgrim set out. As particular routes became well trodden, they became Caminos in their own right.

A number of these Caminos are still known and used today. They include the Caminos Portugués (the Portuguese Ways), the Camino del Norte (the Northern Way, that traces the north coast of Spain before ducking inland to reach Santiago), and the Via de la Plata (the 'Metal' or 'Silver' Way). The latter is one of the more remote and demanding Caminos, crossing central Spain from south to north for over 900 kilometres.

A Slow Walk Across Spain   121

Beyond the Iberian Peninsula, the Caminos begin from different parts of Europe and approach Spain via France's four main Caminos – through Orléans, Vézelay, Le Puy and Arles. All of these Caminos cross the Pyrenees from France into Spain and flow into one as they turn westward across Spain to Santiago de Compostela. Since it is fed by the Caminos of France, it is known as the Camino Francés or 'French Way'.

Nowadays, when people refer to the Camino de Santiago, or the Way of Saint James, they usually mean the Camino Francés.

The map on page 13 shows the more well known of these ancient Caminos and the points at which they join with the Camino Francés. Almost all of the overland pilgrimage routes to Santiago de Compostela link up with this main arterial path at some point.

For most of its journey, the Camino Francés hugs a path about 100 kilometres inland from Spain's north coast, separated from it by several spectacular ranges of mountains. Both mysterious and protective, these jagged, often snow-capped peaks become a quietly familiar presence along the right-hand horizon of the Way.

MYTH AND MIRACLE:
the 'romantic' history of the Camino

We began our first Camino at the small hamlet of Roncesvalles on the Spanish side of the Pyrenees – the much-celebrated range of mountains that separates the Iberian Peninsula from the rest of Europe.

When I walked the Camino for the first time, I knew only its simple, romantic history. As for the history and culture of Spain itself I knew virtually nothing beyond what I'd learned at school here in Australia. It wasn't much more than bullfights and the Spanish Armada.

Yet, to me, Spain was mysterious and exotic in a way that no other country in Europe could match. Given that the south coast of Spain is only a stone's throw from the north coast of Africa, I also felt that Spain had more of the characteristics of that continent. Through my childhood I had imagined it to be like an Aladdin's cave where gold and precious stones beckoned from the gloom. I admit that this impression had far more basis in my fascination with midday movies like *Ali Baba and the Forty Thieves* that were regular Sunday television fare in Australia in the 1960s, than in any formal study of Spanish history.

Before walking the Camino for the first time, I tried to do a little homework on its history. Most of the guidebooks I read before leaving for Spain told a fairly consistent story of the origin of the Camino de Santiago. It goes something like this:

In the first century after the death of Christ, the apostles were sent to various destinations to spread the word of Christianity. Saint James, a cousin of Jesus and one of the apostles, drew the straw for the Iberian Peninsula. It seems to have been a fairly short straw, for by the time he returned to the Holy Land a year later, it is said that he had made only four converts.

On returning to Judea in 44 AD, James was martyred at the hands of Herod Agrippa. At this time, Christianity was seen as a small but annoying cult, and its followers unworthy of respect. To add insult to injury, Herod refused to allow James' followers to give him a Christian burial and so his remains were flung outside the city walls to be eaten by vultures and wild dogs.

Somehow, the Christians in Jerusalem managed to rescue the remains of Saint James. It is said that they placed these remains in a stone boat and then set it adrift in the Mediterranean Sea.

At this point an element of the miraculous joins with myth. As the stone boat carrying the remains of Saint James drifted at sea, an angel descended from heaven and began to guide the boat westward. This is the point where, in primary school, I'd be asking really annoying questions like "… but why didn't the stone boat sink?" and be answered by a steely-eyed nun with "Karen, just have faith!"

The angel guided the stone boat westward until it reached the Pillars of Hercules (now the Strait of Gibraltar), then nudged it up the west coast of Spain, to Iria Flavia in the area we now know as Galicia.

Now entering this tale of angels and epic ocean voyages is the image of the humble scallop shell. One story relates that, as the boat neared the shore of Galicia, a gallant young man galloped into the sea on his horse to rescue the remains of the saint. When all emerged from the waters, the rider, his horse and the remains of the saint were covered in scallop shells.

Perhaps this is not so far-fetched as, even now, scallop shells are plentiful on the beaches and menus of Galicia and northern Spain. They are always called, in one way or another, depending on the region and the language, 'shells of Saint James'. The scallop shell became the symbol of Saint James and of the Camino de Santiago and statues of Saint James the Pilgrim show a scallop shell holding back the wide brim of his felt hat.

Once the remains of Saint James had been retrieved from the sea, they were taken inland and buried by his followers (perhaps they were those who James had converted) in a simple crypt in the side of a hill. Some accounts say that two of his followers were buried with him. Whether alone or in company, there he lay, forgotten and undisturbed for the next 750 years.

One night in 810 AD a simple Galician hermit named Pelayo noticed a strange group of stars. It was clear that they were of divine origin and were guiding him to a particular hillside. Pelayo dug where the stars directed him and is said to have discovered the ancient remains of Saint James.

Pelayo ran to tell the local Bishop, Theodimious, who hurried to tell the Catholic King of Spain, Alphonso II, who in turn rushed to tell Pope Leo III and the Roman Emperor Charlemagne. Immediately a small chapel was built at the site and named Santiago de Compostela.

Some historians claim that the name of the city derives from the Latin 'composita tella', or 'burial ground'. (It is known that there is a cemetery of Roman origin beneath the foundations of the cathedral of Santiago de Compostela). I prefer the interpretation based on the Latin 'campus stellae' or 'field of stars'. Santiago de Compostela then translates as 'Saint James of the Field of Stars'. The Camino Francés is also referred to as the 'Milky Way' because that astral highway mirrors its westward path.

The religious fervour that followed the reporting of the discovery of the remains of Saint James can only be imagined in today's more secular world. The medieval psyche and religions were obsessed with the relics of saints and martyrs (whether the full

Saint James the pilgrim

remains of a saint, or just a part of them – a tooth, a fingernail, a strand of hair, a splinter of a cross or a piece of cloth or jewellery) and with their power to extend a spiritual benefit or blessing to those who came in contact with them.

As word spread throughout Christian Europe, seeing and touching the saintly remains at the heart of Santiago's cathedral became the goal of thousands and then millions of pilgrims. The Cult of Saint James had begun. Pilgrims would have come in trickles at first but the stream soon became a flood.

This was the story I had in my mind as I set out from Roncesvalles on my first Camino. By the time I had reached Santiago de Compostela, I was aware that the history of the pilgrimage was much more complex and that there was more to Saint James than the humble pilgrim.

THE PILGRIM AND THE MOOR SLAYER: the two faces of Saint James

My curiosity about the history of the Camino was stirred by a number of clues that I noticed as I walked the pilgrimage for the first time. The Camino is famous not only for its architecture, but also for the many works of art dedicated to Saint James and to the pilgrimage. These paintings and sculptures range from ornate works commissioned in historic times to simple murals painted by local townsfolk. What made me more and more curious was that Saint James is represented in the villages and churches across northern Spain in two very different ways.

The first is the one I had expected, Saint James the Pilgrim, wearing sandals and dressed in a simple cloak and a felt hat, its brim turned back and held in place by the scallop shell. Attached to his belt is a dried and hollowed gourd for carrying water. Across one shoulder hangs a simple cloth bag for carrying his food and a few possessions. In his hand he holds a long, wooden staff. This incarnation of Saint James is one that exudes peace, patience and goodwill – a fitting patron for such a pilgrimage.

A few weeks into the pilgrimage, I began to notice another depiction of Saint James in churches and above the doorways of some of the ancient pilgrim hospitals. This is a far less peaceful Saint James. In full battle dress, he sits astride an enormous, rearing,

A Slow Walk Across Spain   125

white stallion. In his raised right hand is a battle sword, in the other he holds aloft a snowy white banner emblazoned with a blood-red cross, and he looks down in ferocious satisfaction at the slain, beheaded and wounded foes at his feet.

When I initially realised that this recurring image was Saint James and not some other famous Spanish warrior like El Cid, I was genuinely confused. When did Saint James step out of his pilgrim garb and into the armour of a warrior? Was he a pilgrim who became a warrior or vice versa? Was this the same Saint James who visited the Iberian Peninsula as a humble evangelist? Who was he fighting against and why?

Finding the answers to all these questions took me a year or two. Given that I didn't know what I was looking for, I probably took a fairly circuitous route that involved a few dead ends and false leads. But it also involved some very satisfying sleuthing, including a couple of days in the stacks of Sydney University

Santiago Matamoros (Saint James the Moor Slayer)

Library, where I had that wonderful experience of losing all track of time amongst the books as I pieced together the puzzle of the Camino and the two faces of Saint James.

What I found was that the history of the Camino de Santiago is intricately linked to the Christian and Islamic history of the Iberian Peninsula. The 'infidels' beneath the hooves of Saint James' horse are the Moors, the Muslim invaders of Spain, and Saint James the Pilgrim has metamorphosed into 'Santiago Matamoros' or 'Saint James the Moor Slayer'. It's hard to conjure up two more disparate images than that of a sandalled pilgrim and a saddled avenger!

These two faces of Saint James developed in the 750 years between his death and the discovery of his remains. Things may have been very quiet around the Galician hillside where Saint James lay buried and forgotten, but there was a lot going on in the rest of Spain in that 750 years between 44 and 810 AD. The Iberian Peninsula not only changed its name, but also its political, religious and racial identities, numerous times. What we now call Spain and Portugal played both host and enemy to a diversity of invaders, rulers and refugees. It was a shining example of the best of human society, but also of the horrific consequences of intolerance and fanaticism.

ONE THOUSAND YEARS OF HISTORY

Up until about 400 AD, Spain (or Hispania), along with almost all the lands that bordered the Mediterranean Sea, was part of the Roman Empire. Pilgrims walking the Camino today will still find the rounded cobbles of Roman roads and the beautiful grey stone spans of Roman bridges underfoot. These were part of the infrastructure that supported the garrisons of Roman soldiers and the merchant trading that Roman conquest and civilisation brought to Spain.

HISPANIA: Rome's western frontier

Because it formed the far western frontier of the Roman Empire, the Iberian Peninsula was in many ways ignored and under-resourced compared with the more populated centres closer to Rome. Hispania shared in far fewer of the urban advantages enjoyed by the Roman lands further east and instead, provided the empire with primary resources such as grain and metal. While the upper classes enjoyed the wealth and prestige of their connection with Rome, the middle classes were overtaxed and the lower classes overworked. Dissatisfied subjects who did not support their rulers meant that Hispania was a weak point in the Roman Empire.

By the 4th century AD, the local languages of pre-Roman Iberia had been largely replaced by a distinctive regional dialect of Latin. It was from this dialect that the Romance language of Spanish (or Castilian) developed. In the Basque country, straddling the Pyrenees in Spain's east, the native language of

The Roman bridge at Puente la Reina

Euskera survived, as did the Gallego language (which has similarities to Portuguese) in western Spain's Galicia.

Until the 4th century, the Roman Empire tolerated all religions on the condition that they accepted the Roman state gods. However, Christianity was steadily spreading throughout the empire and its followers were unwilling to pay homage to the Roman gods. In the year 313 AD, the emperor Constantine granted tolerance to Christianity. Later, the worship of pagan gods was abolished and Christianity became the official religion of the Roman Empire.

Around the end of the 4th century, the strength of the Roman Empire's western frontier began to falter. The self-indulgent upper classes had relied too heavily and for too long on the lower classes to fill the ranks of the empire's armies and to produce the goods and services to which they'd become accustomed. On the Iberian Peninsula, most of Rome's subjects spent their lives working for the empire, whether as labourers or as tax payers. It was a pretty unequal equation, with Rome gaining far more than it gave and the Roman subjects in Spain living fairly miserable lives.

THE GOTHS ARE COMING!

To make their western flank even more vulnerable, Roman armies stationed in Spain were relying more and more on mercenaries – 'barbarians' from the Germanic tribes to the north, to fill their garrisons. It was these barbarian tribes – the Vandals, Alans, Sueves and particularly the Visigoths – who finally wrested most of Spain from the Roman Empire when they invaded in about 400 AD. They set up an independent kingdom that stretched from the Iberian Peninsula through northern Africa. This Gothic kingdom would continue in Spain until just after 700 AD. In the area to the north of the Pyrenees (what is now France), another Germanic kingdom, that of the Franks, had taken hold.

Under the Visigoths, the Iberian Peninsula was relatively cohesive – something that is always remarkable when it comes to that part of the world. The Goths were Christians and had lived for centuries in an uneasy neighbourliness with Rome. They differed from the Romans in that their invasion of the Peninsula involved bringing with them their families and animals – their communities. The local Hispano-Romans put up no fight against the Visigoths and, apart from the odd skirmish with armies of disgruntled Romans, they ruled more or less for the next 300 years.

A BOLT FROM THE BLUE: the arrival of the Moors

Most historical accounts of the events that followed use terms like 'a bolt from the blue' to evoke their unexpectedness. Suddenly and dramatically, in 711 AD, while the Visigothic King Roderic was busy putting down a revolt in the Pyrenees, Arabs and Berbers invaded from North Africa. The Berbers with their leader, Gebel Tarik, landed first on what was known as the Lion's Rock, now known as Gibraltar – a form of the name of Gebel Tarik.

This hand-shaped doorknocker is of Moorish origin.

King Roderic raced south with a substantial army, but was overcome by the invaders at a place on the south coast of Spain known as Jerez de la Frontera. Musa, the Governor of Africa, described the Arab victory as being like '... the meeting of the nations on the Day of Judgement.' The Christian army had been overcome by a Muslim army – one of the most important turning points in the history of Spain.

The invaders took only two years to gain control of almost all of the Iberian Peninsula. The Islamic dominions already extended from Central Asia, through the Middle East and North Africa, and now had pushed up through the Iberian Peninsula to the Pyrenees.

The new rulers called this land 'Al-Andalus' and it became part of the largest empire the world had ever seen. Its rulers, the 'caliphs', were regarded as the religious and civil successors to the prophet Mohammed and for the next 700 years the Arab caliphate would, to a greater and then lesser extent, maintain its hold on Al-Andalus.

Not all who were subjected to the dominion of the Moors felt obliged to rebel. Most ordinary Christian citizens had heard of the tolerance of the Moors and so put up no resistance, and the Jewish people of Sefarad (the Jewish word for Spain) had been persecuted by the Visigoths and seen as heretics by the Catholics and so were probably welcoming of their new rulers.

Groups such as the Christians and Jews were able to live relatively peacefully in Islamic Spain, the different cultures influencing and enriching each other. This was particularly the case in the larger cities of the south, such as Cordoba. In the 9th and 10th centuries AD, it was not only the capital of Islamic Al-Andalus but was also the largest and most sophisticated city in western Europe.

The cultural phenomenon of Al-Andulus waxed and waned over its 700 years but Islamic influence certainly bestowed many gifts that are still evident today in Spanish and western European culture. These include knowledge from many fields, and translations of the classics that had come to the Arab world from ancient Greek culture. It was through Al-Andalus that knowledge of Aristotle was dispersed through medieval Europe.

Many historians agree that Spain under the Moors was, for at least some of their rule, a tolerant and highly cultivated society.

One small but very significant group were not so disposed to welcome the new Muslim rulers. The former Christian ruling class of Visigothic Spain were not at all happy to be governed by the 'infidel'. They retreated to the most inaccessible area of their peninsula, the mountainous and sparsely populated north west.

By the early 9th century AD, the Moors had taken most of Spain and had even pushed on further into Europe, crossing the Pyrenees into France. As they headed towards Paris, they were turned back at what many historians call the most crucial European battle of medieval times – the battle of Limoges. The Moors withdrew back across the Pyrenees to consolidate their rule in Spain. The Christian countries north of the Pyrenees no doubt breathed a sigh of relief and relegated the Moors to the relative physical and psychological safety of 'over the Pyrenees'.

ASTURIAS: the stronghold of Christian Spain

Meanwhile, in north-west Spain, the Christian refugees of the Gothic and Roman ruling classes grouped themselves around the town of Covadonga. This remnant group of Spanish Christians would eventually become the Christian kingdom of Asturias – a lone stronghold of Christianity in a land governed by Muslims.

Asturias was a wet, cold and mountainous region and the Moors, it seems, considered it not worth the trouble of defeating. The Asturians, having far more to gain, persisted in extending their kingdom and by the end of the 9th century AD, had won back a large part of northern Spain, including the western region of Galicia.

RECONQUISTA: taking back Spain for Christianity

This winning back of the Iberian Peninsula by the Christians had its small but hugely significant beginnings in 718 AD.

The Moors had sent yet another skirmishing party to subdue the Christians. In this particular battle, the Christians were victorious. The Moors would not have been too troubled by this

The Cruz Ferro (Iron Cross) in the Mountains of Leon, just south of the Principality of Asturias

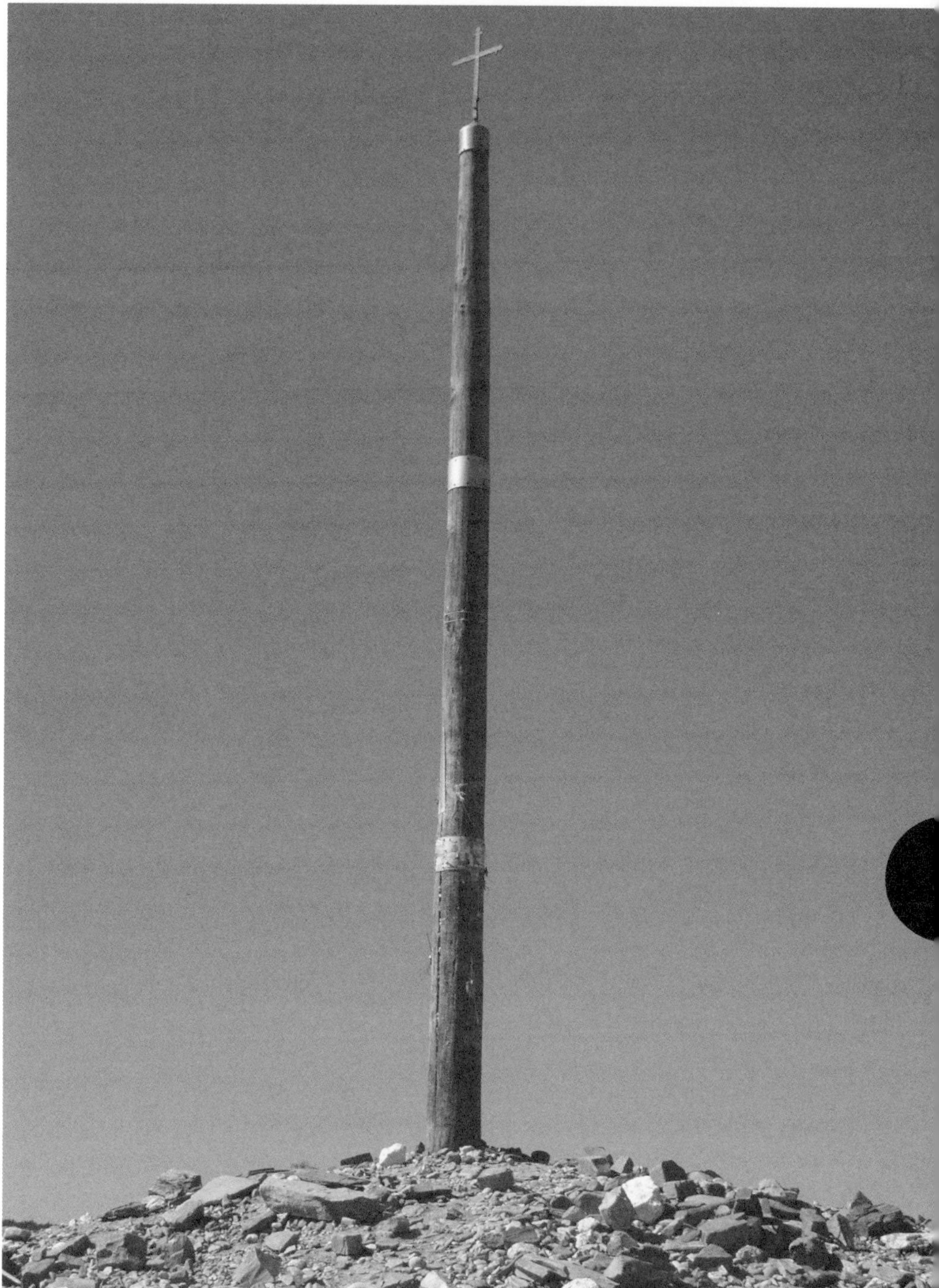

minor defeat in a region that mattered little to them. From a Christian perspective, however, this victory went down in history as the beginning of the 'Reconquista', the Christian reconquest of Spain. It would take 750 years to complete, but it had begun.

The other Christian kingdoms of western Europe largely turned their backs on the Christians of Spain. Yes, the 'infidel' were on Europe's doorstep but the Muslims had been defeated on French soil and had retreated safely behind the barrier of the Pyrenees. Out of sight, out of mind.

The Christian minority in the north of Spain was fanatical in its commitment to rid Spain of the 'Muslim infidel', yet it seemed that this was a battle that was impossible to win. Even though the Christians had won one small battle, how could such a relatively small population take on the might of its Muslim foe?

The rebellious Christians were further disadvantaged by the fact that the Moors held, in the great mosque of Cordoba, relics of their prophet Mohammed. Cordoba and the mosque that held the relics of the Prophet were the jewels in the crown of Al-Andalus. In his book *The Road to Santiago*, Walter Starkie describes the architectural and psychological significance of the great mosque in Cordoba:

> ... the great Abderrahman I founded the mosque in Cordoba on the site of a Visigothic church, which had itself been built on the ruins of a Roman temple dedicated to Janus. To this house he gave the name of Zeca or House of Purification, and he resolved that it should rival Mecca, and become the sacred city of the Western Mohammedan world. In the course of the centuries it was to become, after the Kaaba, the largest and most beautiful building of Islam, with its nineteen gateways of bronze, its four thousand seven hundred lamps of perfumed oil, its roof supported by twelve hundred columns of porphyry, jasper and many-coloured marbles. But what drew the attention of the world towards the mosque was not its artistic splendours but the realisation that the shrine contained some of the bones of the Prophet Mahomet himself. (p.19)

In a time when the cult of relic worship was at its height, the remains of the Prophet at Cordoba gave enormous psychological power to the Moors. Muslim soldiers believed that if they died in battle, they would gain automatic entry into paradise. This psychological weapon made them formidable foes, and with relics of the Prophet on the very ground they were defending, it would seem they were invincible.

The fledgling Christian kingdom of Asturias in north-west Spain required an equally potent motivation if its soldiers were to overcome such a fearless enemy.

DIVINE INTERVENTION: the discovery of the remains of Saint James

The answer to the prayers of Spain's Christians came in 812 AD when, miraculously, the remains of Saint James the Apostle, cousin of Jesus and martyr for Christianity, were unearthed in north-west Spain.

Suddenly, the attention of all Christians of western Europe and England turned to this backward and forgotten corner of Spain. Here was a sign from God and a reason for the Christian world to offer both moral and economic support to Asturias' war against the Moors of Al-Andalus. Almost straight away, both pilgrims and crusading soldiers set out from all over Europe, towards the north-west corner of Spain. The paths that their footsteps created as they made their way to Santiago de Compostela would become the Caminos or 'ways' of Saint James.

The power of the presence of Saint James grew as a number of miracles began to occur. By far the most important was in 845 AD, some 30 years after the discovery of the remains of Saint James.

In an enforced deference to the power of the Moors, the Christian king of Asturias was obliged to hand over a yearly tribute of 100 maidens to the Moorish caliph. In 845 AD the Christians refused. Of course the caliph, Abderrahman II, had no choice but to declare war and in the ensuing battle the Christians were defeated. They took refuge on nearby Mount Clavijo and prepared to fight again.

It was during this second battle that Saint James is said to have appeared. He was mounted on a white charger, flying a snow-white banner that bore a blood-red cross. In his right hand he brandished a flashing sword. It is said that in that one battle, Saint James, in the form of Santiago Matamoros (the Moor

Slayer), single-handedly slew 60,000 Moors and won the battle for the Christians. They vowed to honour him henceforth as their patron saint by paying the church at Santiago a bushel of corn or its equivalent value in wine for every acre of ploughed land. This law was not revoked until the year 1812.

A BATTLE WON, ANOTHER BEGINS: the fight for Catholic Spain

The chapel (and eventually the cathedral) of Santiago de Compostela rapidly grew in importance as a destination for pilgrims. In the early days of the pilgrimage, in the 9th and 10th centuries, however, there wasn't much to make a pilgrim's journey easy or comfortable. Until the 'ways' of Saint James became more established, pilgrims had to be as self-sufficient as possible. They had to rely on the food they could gather from the forests and fields, and on the goodwill of the few locals along the way.

Statue of a weary pilgrim outside the old pilgrim hospital in Leon

To add to the dangers of the journey, the Christian kingdom of Asturias and the growing city of Santiago de Compostela were by no means safely separated from Islamic Al-Andalus. In 997 AD, the Muslim caliph, Almanzor, and his army entered the city of Santiago and razed it and its cathedral to the ground.

History reflects the perspective of historians, and the accounts of the sacking of Santiago are no exception. Some accounts give credit to Almanzor's mercy. They claim that on entering the cathedral, he found an old monk saying his prayers at the tomb of Saint James. Rather than kill the monk and destroy the remains of the saint, Almanzor set up a guard to ensure the monk's prayers and the remains of Saint James were undisturbed. The Christian accounts of Almanzor's sacking of Santiago claim that, after destroying the cathedral, he was unable to find the remains of Saint James because he was confounded by a brilliant light that surrounded the tomb.

THE SPANISH CRUSADE

During the 11th century, with the help of the hero warrior, El Cid, Santiago de Compostela was recaptured for Christian Asturias. Eventually it became part of the great triumvirate of Christian pilgrimage sites along with Jerusalem and Rome, the burial sites of Jesus Christ and Saint Peter. Santiago had an important similarity to the resting place of Jesus – Jerusalem. Like Jerusalem, Santiago was in a land still held by the 'infidel' and so was a city that needed to be liberated by the great Crusades. The knights who chose to fight for Christian Spain were exempt from making the far longer and more dangerous crusade to the Holy Land and many crusaders from eastern Europe chose to fight for Santiago.

ALL OF HUMANITY ON THE ROAD: the pilgrims of the Middle Ages

While the Camino and the cathedral at Santiago de Compostela attracted the political manoeuvres of Church and State, pilgrims continued to set out to walk to Santiago from all over western Europe. They came from as far afield as Scandanavia, Belgium, Germany, France, England, Switzerland, Italy and Greece.

Historians have estimated that up to one in three Christian Europeans walked to Santiago (and usually back home again!) in medieval times. Most travelled on foot, some with a horse or donkey and a few, who had enough money, either travelled with an entourage or even paid someone else to walk the Camino for them. (It seems that religious

A Slow Walk Across Spain   137

rewards were transferable if one was willing to pay a price.) From popes, kings and cardinals to poor vagabonds, the pilgrimage reflected every level of the social order. Pilgrims tended to travel in spring and summer, often in large groups as a means of keeping safe.

Many pilgrims received donations from friends and acquaintances wanting to help them on their journey. Those who helped pilgrims by giving money, food or other comfort believed that they would also acquire spiritual merit and so a pilgrim could expect to encounter kindness and support from villagers along the way.

WHAT REMAINS: the worship of relics

The vast majority of those who walked the Camino were Christian, but during the times when any religious relics were viewed as the divine made evident, followers of other religions (including Islam and Judaism) viewed the remains of Saint James in Santiago as worthy of pilgrimage. This may seem strange now, but relics were not necessarily exclusive to their particular religions when it came to attracting pilgrims.

As the pilgrimage to Santiago grew in importance and popularity, towns and cities that lay along the many 'ways' or 'Caminos' sought to attract more pilgrims by securing relics and installing them in their churches and cathedrals. Relics meant more pilgrims, and more pilgrims meant more trade and commerce. Pilgrimage provided a form of tourism mixed with spiritual merit – a very popular blend during the Middle Ages.

Pilgrims' reasons for undertaking their journeys ranged right across the spectrum of human motivation. Some walked to make amends for past misdeeds or to honour a promise to a dying relative. Others walked to give thanks for a perceived blessing of health or fortune. Some walked out of simple wanderlust – the urge to travel and see foreign lands. They shared the road with bandits and criminals, some of whom were on the run and disguised as pilgrims. All was set to music by the minstrels or 'juglares' who played and sang the many songs that became famous on the Camino.

In the early years of the Camino, a pilgrimage was guaranteed to be a life and death experience. The medieval pilgrim couldn't catch a plane, train or bus to their point of departure. Instead, having said their goodbyes to family and friends, they would simply walk out their front door and head in the direction of Santiago de Compostela on the roads and paths available to them. Their goodbyes would have been heartfelt, as their return was by no means certain. Lying in wait on the road ahead of them lay inclement weather, injury, disease, wolves, bears, wild boars, bandits and untrustworthy ferrymen, and pilgrims also had a real fear of Satan in all his guises.

Tales of the perils of medieval pilgrimage abound. One of the earliest written records is the *Codex Calixtinus* edited by Aimery Picaud, a priest from Poitiers in France. It is probably the first tourist guide ever to be written in western Europe. It was published in Latin in about 1130 as the *Liber Sancti Jacobi* (The Book of Saint James), when the Way of Saint James was already well established. It gave even greater publicity to the pilgrimage. Walter Starkie observes that it was written as "… a manual of propaganda, in order to boost the pilgrimage to the tomb of Saint James."

Aimery Picaud's descriptions of the regions and peoples encountered on the pilgrimage confirm that nothing much has changed when it comes to humans' reactions to people they deem 'foreigners' and lands they think strange. Here are a few observations from that medieval travel guide which might as well have been entitled 'There's No Place Like Home':

… of the region of Bordeaux:

> It is a desolate country where everything is missing. There is neither bread, nor wine, nor meat, nor fish: no water and no springs; the villages are few and far between in this sandy country, where, however, there is a fair amount of honey and millet; and there are pigs.

… of toll collectors:

> These people, frankly, should be consigned to the devil. They actually go in front of the pilgrims with two or three sticks to extort from them by force unjust fees, and if any traveller refuses to give in to their demands and give them money they hit them with their sticks and take away from them their taxes; and greatly swearing they even rummage in their trousers.

... of boatmen:
> And cursed be their boatmen. In fact, although these rivers are quite narrow, these terrible boatmen have the practice of demanding from each person who goes from one side to the other, whether he is rich or poor, a sum of money and for a horse they extort four pieces by force. Now the boat is small; it is only made of a single tree trunk and can hardly take a horse. Not only that, but after having received money the ferrymen take such a large number of pilgrims that the boat upsets and the pilgrims are drowned and then it is that these boatmen are wickedly happy because they take from the dead all their things.

... of the people of the Pyrenees:
> These people are badly dressed and they eat and drink badly ... the entire household, servant and master, maid and mistress, all eat from the same cauldron in which all the food has been thrown. They eat with their hands without using spoons and all drink from the same goblet. When one watches them eating one is reminded of dogs or pigs gulping gluttonously; and listening to them talk sounds like dogs barking.

... of Galicia:
> The people of Galicia are, above all the other uncultured races of Spain, those who are closest to our French race in their customs; but they are, it is said, inclined to anger and chicanery.

Oh dear, the trials of travel to foreign lands!

Fortunately for the millions of pilgrims who walked the Camino, support and comfort in the form of accommodation and medical assistance became more common as the Camino grew in popularity and religious and political importance. But the importance of the Camino also brought with it the playing out of the conflicts between the Spanish and Franco-Roman sects of the Catholic Church.

By the 11th century, religious orders such as the French monks of Cluny had been sent to set up their abbeys, monasteries and pilgrim hospitals along the Camino and were ministering to the multitude of pilgrims who came to their doors. The influence of

The old pilgrim hospital (now a Parador) in Leon

the monks of Cluny, and hence of the French Catholic Church, would become critical to the changing shape of Christian Spain. It would result in the Mozarabic Catholic ritual (with its roots in Spain's early Roman history and influences from Toledo and the Visigothic church) being replaced by the liturgy favoured by Pope Gregory and the Church in Rome and France.

... IN FOURTEEN HUNDRED AND NINETY-TWO: the victory of Christianity

My schoolgirl knowledge of the Iberian Peninsula wasn't much more than the repetition of the rhyme 'In fourteen hundred and ninety-two, Columbus sailed the ocean blue.' Thanks to the Camino and the curiosity about all things Iberian that it engendered, I now know more of the extent of that date's significance.

In 1492, Spain's newly-married monarchs, Ferdinand and Isabella, took control of the city of Granada and brought the Reconquista to its uncompromising end. They ordered the expulsion from what was now a totally Catholic Spain, of all Muslims, Jews and Gypsies. Like many such 'cleansings' before and since, it was a violent and relentless process. It was in 1492 that Boabdil, the last Muslim ruler of Granada, left the Alhambra palace, so leaving all of Spain to Christian rule for the first time in over 800 years.

Over the next century or so, Spain's Christian rulers would do their best to wipe all vestiges of Moorish influence from the peninsula. The 'Moriscos', those Moors who had claimed a conversion to Christianity in order to remain in their homeland, were eventually banished or massacred.

In his book, *Ghosts of Spain*, Giles Tremlett asks:

> Should Spain be defined as a proudly Roman Catholic nation that emerged, or re-emerged, from a valiant eight-century battle against Islam? Or should it, as the historian Americo Castro first proposed decades ago, think of itself as being forged from a historic encounter between religions and cultures, including both Islam and Judaism?

WALKING IN THE FOOTSTEPS OF HISTORY: ancient and modern pilgrims

I'm sometimes asked why I walked the same Camino twice. In fact, many people walk the same Camino more than once. I guess it's true of any walking journey we've enjoyed. It's not unusual to want to walk it again. Given that we'll always encounter differences in weather, the people we meet, the way we feel, and countless other variables, no Camino will ever be the same.

The research and 'historical sleuthing' I'd done between our first and second Caminos gave me a wider perspective on my second trek. This time, I felt that I was looking at the towns, villages and countryside with a new awareness.

Everywhere I could see the traces of history and of the powers and politics that had played out around the path. The history of the Camino is one of peaceful pilgrimage, yes, but of so much more. It is also a history of turmoil, and of the push and shove of cultures and religions as they compete for influence.

I've also been asked if I was disappointed or disheartened when I found out about James the 'warrior saint' after walking a pilgrimage that I thought was devoted to a figure who represented peaceful contemplation – Saint James the Pilgrim.

Human history is rarely wholly 'good' or 'evil' when all its layers are revealed. For me, it is a fascinating human irony that the humble garb of Saint James the Pilgrim can be cast aside to reveal a veritable caped crusader – Santiago Matamoros, or Saint James the Moor Slayer.

As much of this book has shown, there are many lessons to be learned from hindsight. Relinquishing a heavy pack, along with a controlling mindset, is a start. There's no telling where sharing a long path, in the company of diverse companions, will lead.

The cathedral at Santiago de Compostela

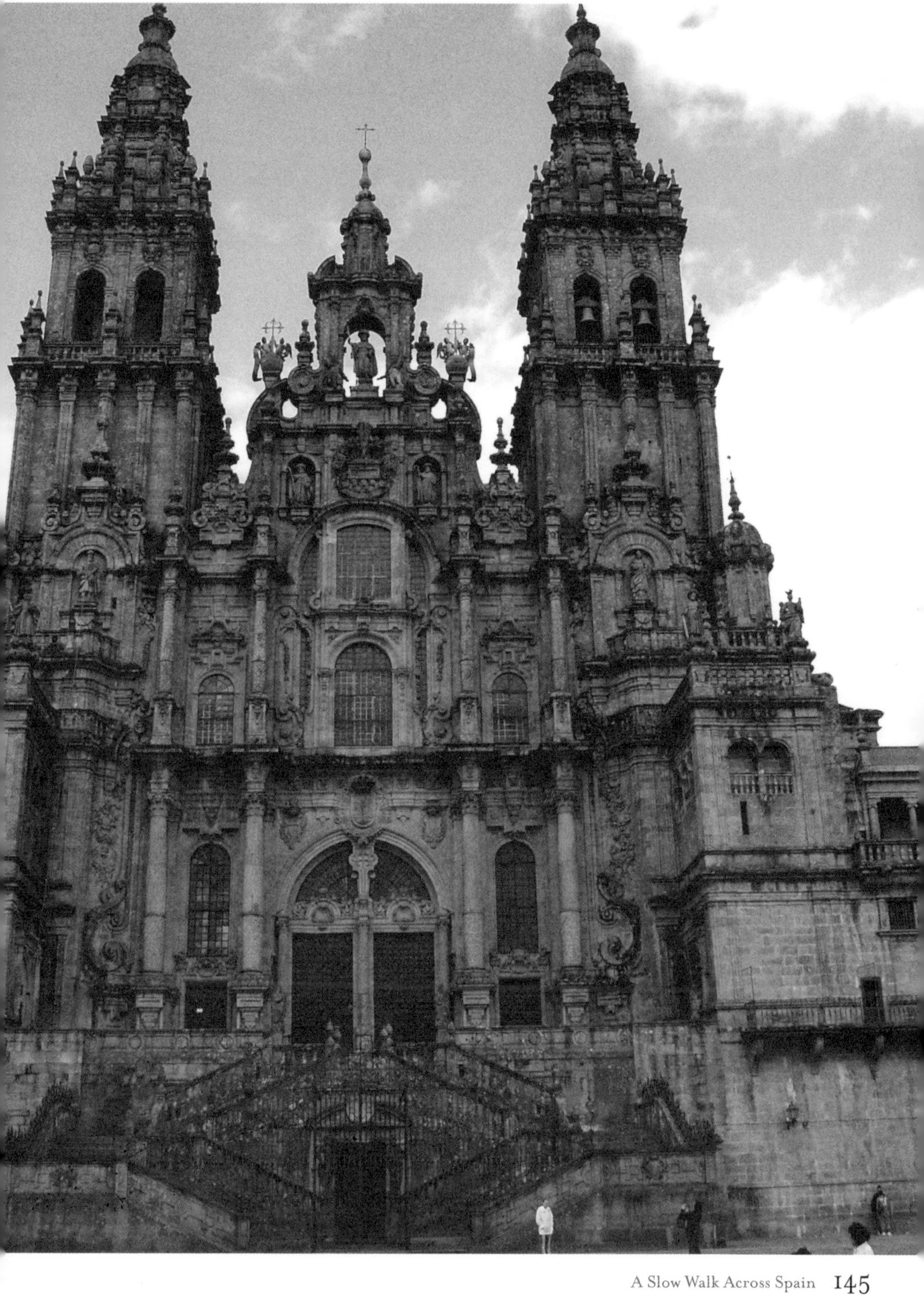

Tarta de Santiago

Serves 8-10

Here is a recipe for the famous 'Tarta de Santiago' or Saint James' cake. With its surface decorated with an icing sugar stencil of Saint James' sword, this traditional Galician cake acknowledges the 'warrior saint'.

You might want to add a symbol of a walking pole to keep things in balance.

INGREDIENTS

250g whole almonds, with skins
6 large eggs, separated
200g caster sugar
large pinch of ground cinnamon
icing sugar, for dusting
butter, for greasing
fine sea salt
24cm deep spring form cake tin, greased with butter and base-lined
(slash the paper so it reaches 3cm up the sides)

METHOD

Using a clean coffee grinder or a spice grinder, grind the almonds until fine, with no lumps.

Put the egg whites and a pinch of salt in a bowl and whisk until soft peaks form. Whisk in half the sugar, one tablespoon at a time, to stabilize the whites.

Whisk the yolks with the remaining sugar and cinnamon until thick and the volume has increased. The mixture should leave a trail when you raise the whisk from the bowl.

Fold the ground almonds into the egg yolk mixture. Fold in a little of the whites to loosen the mixture, then fold in the remainder.

Spoon into the tin and bake in a preheated oven at 180C (350F) for about 45 mins until cooked, golden and firm but springy.

Check after 35 mins – if it's over-browning, cover with greaseproof paper and continue baking.

Remove from the oven and let cool in the tin on a wire rack for 10 mins then unmold onto the rack to cool completely.

Dust with icing sugar using a stencil of Saint James' sword if you wish.

Here is a stencil of Saint James' sword to simply cut out and place on top of finished cake and dust with icing sugar.

A Slow Walk Across Spain

"CAMINO DE SANTIAGO"
Fecha:
El Desvan del
Villalcázar de
(Palencia)
Tfno. y Fax 979
Fecha:
Fecha:
Peregrinos de Atapuerca
Fecha:
HOSTAL
DE SAN
LEON
2004
Fecha:
SAN BOL
BURGOS
Fecha:
ALBERGUE
Fecha:
Fecha:
VILLARMENTERO DE CAMPOS
Y LA...
Fecha:
REFUGIO DE
LEON
NON
NOBIS
Fecha:

pilgrim [*pil*gRim] *n* one who for religious reasons visits sacred places, shrines *etc*; (*ar*) traveller; **P. Fathers** band of Puritans who in 1620 left England and founded a colony in Plymouth, New England.

pilgrimage [*pil*gRimij] *n* journey to a sacred spot, shrine *etc*; journey to a place revered for its associations; (*fig*) human lifetime.

BIBLIOGRAPHY

REFERENCES:

Layton, T.A., *The Way of Saint James or The Pilgrims' Road to Santiago de Compostela*, Allen & Unwin, London, 1976 (including the quotes from Aimery Picaud's *Codex Calixtinus*).

Starkie, Walter, *The Road to Santiago: Pilgrims of Saint James*, John Murray, London, 1957

Tremlett, Giles, *Ghosts of Spain: Travels Through a Country's Hidden Past*, Faber and Faber, London, 2007

SUGGESTED READING

These are just a few favourite titles, there are MANY more ...

Christmas, Jane, *What the Psychic Told the Pilgrim*, East Street Publications, Millswood, South Australia, 2007

Crow, John A., *Spain: the Root and the Flower*, University Of California Press, Berkeley, California, 2005

Kevin, Tony, *Walking the Camino: a Modern Pilgrimage to Santiago*, Scribe, Melbourne, 2007

Kurlansky, Mark, *The Basque History of the World*, Vintage (Random House), London, 2000

Nooteboom, Cees, *Roads to Santiago: Detours and Riddles in the Lands and History of Spain*, The Harvill Press (Random House), London, 1997

Rupp, Joyce, *Walk in a Relaxed Manner: Life Lessons from the Camino*, Orbis Books, New York, 2005

SUGGESTED GUIDEBOOKS

Bissett, William, ed., *Pilgrim Guides to Spain: 1 Camino Francés*, Confraternity of Saint James, London (updated annually)

Brierley, John, *A Pilgrim's Guide to the Camino de Santiago: St Jean Pied de Port – Santiago de Compostela*, Findhorn Press, Forres, Scotland, 2008

Davies, Bethan, and Cole, Ben, *Walking the Camino de Santiago: from St Jean Pied de Port to Santiago de Compostela and on to Finisterre*, Pili Pala Press, Vancouver, 2004

FOR CYCLISTS:

Higginson, John, *The Way of Saint James: a Cyclist's Guide*, Cicerone Press, Milnthorpe, UK, 2009

USEFUL WEBSITES

http://www.caminocalling.com
Karen Manwaring's website. An absolute must!

http://www.csj.org.uk/
The Confraternity of Saint James website. Their excellent guidebooks can be purchased online.

http://www.caminosantiago.com
A comprehensive site that includes the useful Pilgrims' Forum

http://www.caminolinks.co.uk
This site links to most English language sites about the Camino.

http://www.eurail.com/
Trains in Europe

http://www.paradores-spain.com/
Paradors are historic, luxury hotels in Spain

For any other web information, a Google search of a particular subject will deliver many other sites to explore.

THANK YOU

All our Camino and close friends who shared the journey with us

Lin Tobias for her unique design work and project management

Peta Murray for her inspirational guidance and editing

Josie Ryan for her most gorgeous web design

Lynn Matheson for her ongoing support and organisational expertise

Clare 'Hawkeye' Williamson for her attention to detail

All those who read the manuscript in its many incarnations, including Fran Madigan, Delia Bradshaw, Anna Walker, Joanna Szabo, Effie Konstantopoulos, Carmel Fenton, Jane Murphy and Louise Graves

Chris Falk and Kate Morris from Alexander Education in Melbourne for their invaluable input re all things Yoga and Alexander Technique

Carl Ridgeway, Ralph Hadden, Cath Tyler, Jan Batty, Dr Denise Wild and Dr Nick Nicolettou for keeping me in shape

Toula Nicolettou for her encouragement and friendship

… and to Angela Nicolettou for her curiosity, courage, adventurousness and good company.

NOTES ON THE FONTS:

MINION is the name of a typeface designed by Robert Slimbach in 1990 for Adobe Systems. The name comes from the traditional naming system for type sizes, in which minion is between nonpareil and brevier. It is inspired by late Renaissance-era type.

DIN, an acronym for the German Deutsches Institut für Normung (German Institute for Standardization), and the name of an increasingly large realist sans-serif typeface family. The earliest version of a DIN typeface was released by the D Stempel AG foundry in 1923.

MRS EAVES is a transitional serif typeface designed by Zuzana Licko in 1996, and licensed by Emigre, a typefoundry run by Licko and husband Rudy VanderLans. Mrs Eaves is a revival of the types of English printer and punchcutter John Baskerville, and is related to contemporary Baskerville typefaces.